CLARENCE E. MACARTNEY

The Greatest Questions of the Bible and of Life

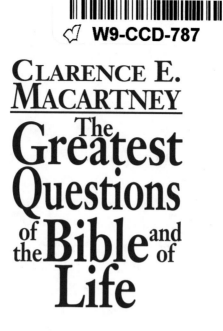

Books by Clarence E. Macartney

Chariots of Fire
Great Women of the Bible
The Greatest Questions of the Bible and of Life
The Greatest Texts of the Bible
The Greatest Words in the Bible and in Human Speech
He Chose Twelve
Paul the Man
Strange Texts but Grand Truths
12 Great Questions About Christ

CLARENCE E. MACARTNEY

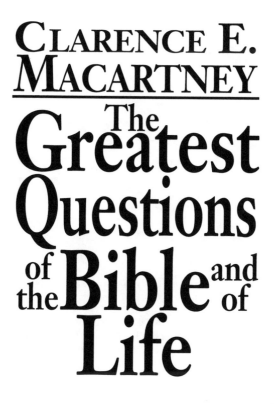

The
Greatest
Questions
of Bible and
the of
Life

kregel
PUBLICATIONS

Grand Rapids, MI 49501

The Greatest Questions of the Bible and of Life
by Clarence E. Macartney.

Published in 1995 by Kregel Publications, a division of
Kregel, Inc., P.O. Box 2607, Grand Rapids, MI 49501.
Kregel Publications provides trusted, biblical publications
for Christian growth and service. Your comments and
suggestions are valued.

Cover Photgraph: Art Jacobs
Cover and book design: Alan G. Hartman

Library of Congress Cataloging-in-Publication Data
Macartney, Clarence Edward Noble, 1879–1957
    The greatest questions of the Bible and of life / Clarence
E. Macartney.
            p.   cm.
    Originally published: New York: Abingdon–Cokesbury
Press, 1948.
    1. Presbyterian Church—Sermons. 2. Sermons, Ameri-
can. I. Title.
BX9178.M172G685   1995   252'.051—dc20   93–36683
                                                                              CIP

ISBN 0-8254-3273-1 (paperback)

            1 2 3 4 5 Printing / Year 99 98 97 96 95

CONTENTS

FOREWORD

One of the most effective ways of teaching doctrine and imparting truth is to ask a question and then answer it. That was the method of some of the famous teachers of the past. Among philosophers it was spoken of as the "Socratic method." But a greater than Socrates has employed this way of teaching truth. The prophets, the psalmist, the apostles, and Jesus Himself made use of it. From that first question of the Bible, "Where art thou?" down to the last, how many great questions are asked in the Bible and answered! Life asks great questions, but life and experience cannot answer them. The Bible alone asks great questions and also answers them.

What I have done in this book is to select some of the great questions of the Bible and state the great answers which the Bible gives. The preacher who preaches on these great questions and gives, not his own answer, but the answer of the Scriptures, will discover, before he is through, that he has struck the major chords of that grandest of all music, the Everlasting Gospel.

CLARENCE E. MACARTNEY

1

WHERE ART THOU?

*"And the Lord God called unto Adam, and said unto
him, Where art thou?"* (Genesis 3:9)

God knew where the man was. He was not asking the question for information, for there is nothing hid from Him. But He wanted the man to answer the question himself.

This was the first question addressed to man at the very dawn of Creation, at the very start of human history, "Where art thou?" It will also be the last question when the history of mankind has been completed. When we have passed through every appointed experience, have faced all the temptations and opportunities of life, have tasted every appointed cup of joy or sorrow, and all the incidents of our mortal probation have been worked out, then, standing before the judgment seat of God, every man must answer this question, "Where art thou?" and give his account to God. In a very real sense you have here the first call to the judgment seat. In these wonderful first chapters in the book of Genesis you have a summary of man's moral history and destiny.

At his creation man was placed in the Garden of Eden, where everything was good and fair. There was only one thing that he was not to do. Of the tree of knowledge of good and evil man was not to eat. In the day that he ate of it he would die. Created in the image of God, man was "free to stand," but also "free to fall." Without that double freedom, that solemn double freedom

9

which is granted to every soul, there can be no development of strength and character. Man chose to fall. When the tempter assured the woman that eating of the fruit of the forbidden tree would be followed by no evil consequences, that it was not true that they would die if they ate thereof, but that, on the contrary, their eyes would be opened and they would become as gods, the woman took of the fruit thereof and did eat, and gave unto her husband with her, and he did eat.

Now look at the consequences. Did they become as gods? No. Instead of that they were afraid and hid themselves amid the trees of the garden. Were their eyes opened? Yes, their eyes were opened, but opened to their nakedness and to their shame, opened to their guilt in the presence of God. Here we have the awakening of guilt and the first reproach of conscience.

The man and woman, knowing that they were naked, sought to cover their nakedness with the leaves which they sewed together; but their moral nakedness—and that is the real point here—they were not able to cover. In the beautiful poetry of the narrative, the man and the woman "heard the voice of the Lord God walking in the garden in the cool of the day." Before this first sin, before his fall, man had free and open converse with God, and how wonderful that must have been! Now that high privilege has been forfeited by sin, and it is only through the chosen Reconciler and Redeemer, the Son of God, that we can have access unto God. From what is said here we judge that in man's innocency the favorite time for God to meet with man and talk with him was in the "cool of the day." But when God came this time, the man and the woman were missing. In their fear and shame they were hiding from the presence of God among the trees of the garden. That is what sin always does. It separates man from God. This is ancient history, but in the lives of millions upon millions who have come and gone since then, this same history, how sin separates man from God, has been repeated.

God called to the man and said unto him, "Where art thou?" The man answered, "I heard thy voice in the garden, and I was afraid, because I was naked, and I hid myself." There and then the first judgment seat was erected. The man and the woman made their plea and acknowledged their disobedience, but blamed another for it—the man, his wife; the woman, the serpent. Each one has judgment pronounced upon him—hard labor and sorrow for the man, pain and suffering for the woman, degradation for the serpent, the expulsion from the garden and the posting at the gates of the garden of the cherubim with the flaming sword which turned every way to keep the way of the Tree of Life. How death has come into the world because sin came first. There was preached the first sermon on the great text, "The wages of sin is death."

Let us give heed for a little to this question which God addressed to man, "Where art thou?" Let us make it the voice of God, as indeed it is, speaking not only to that original man so long ago but also to you and me, "Where art thou?" First, as to the moral law; second, as to thy brother man; and third, as to Jesus Christ the Son of God.

WHERE ART THOU AS TO THE MORAL LAW?

God gave man His law and made with him a covenant. With perfect obedience he was to have perfect blessing. Man chose to disobey God, to break His law, and now he must give his account to God. That question, "Where art thou?" is inevitable. Every wrongdoer has heard it. Here emerges, for the first time in man's history, the sense of shame and the sense of guilt, the two chief effects and consequences of sin. And here also, for the first time, we hear the majestic, solemn, tremendous voice of conscience speaking in the soul of man and rebuking him for what he has done. Among all the proofs of God this perhaps is the most impressive. Man has, as we see here, the sense of right and of wrong. Conscience first warned that they should not break the law of God and eat of the forbidden fruit. Then conscience rebuked them for what they had done. Whence comes this sense of right and wrong? How profound that question, the next question that God asked the man, "Who told thee that thou wast naked?" Ah, yes! man's sense of his nakedness, of his sinfulness! There is something that no laughter, no sneer, no knowledge can dismiss. A sense of a broken law implies a law that was given, and that in turn demands a Lawgiver. Thus in the voice of conscience rebuking man for his sin, asking him where he is and how it stands with him now at this moment, we have the mighty, irrefragable proof of God.

Here conscience made a coward out of man. That is what it has been doing ever since. Sin makes man to hide amid the trees in the garden. Men seek to hide from God amid the trees of pleasure, of business, of politics, and of pursuit of knowledge. But all in vain! That searching and arresting voice penetrates through to every hiding place. "Where art thou?" There is the voice that follows transgression.

This unbreakable relationship which man has with God is either his joy or his misery. Where art thou, then, as to the law of God, taught in the Bible, implanted in the soul? Where art thou as to God in your daily life, in your home, in the business world, in your associations and your pleasures? How searching this question is—"Where art thou?" Is there anything that would make you wish to hide from God? If so, turn from it in repentance and confession, for to be against right, against the moral law, is to have God and the universe against you and only the Devil and his angels for friends.

There is a homely bit of verse by an unknown author entitled "The Man in the Glass." The poetry is mediocre, but the idea is good. It tells a man, after he has won his battle in the struggle of the world and has been acclaimed as a king, to go to the mirror and look at himself and see what *that* man has to say. It is not the opinion of your father or your mother or your wife or your friends which counts, but the verdict of that man who stares back at you from the glass. He is always the man to please; and you can disregard all the rest, for he will be with you clear down to the end.

> And you've passed your most dangerous, difficult test,
>   If the man in the glass is your friend.
> You may fool the whole world down the pathway of years,
>   And get pats on the back as you pass;
> But the final reward will be heartaches and tears,
>   If you have cheated the man in the glass.

How about that man in the glass? What will he say to you

when you look at him, or look at her, tonight when you go to bed or when you rise in the morning? "Where art thou?"

WHERE ART THOU AS TO THY BROTHER MAN?

You might say that the second great question which God addressed to man is that question which God spoke to Cain after he had killed his brother, "Where is Abel thy brother?" It is a question which cannot be dismissed or answered by another question, as guilty Cain tried to answer it and dismiss it when he said, "Am I my brother's keeper?" That is precisely what we are, and there can be no true happy and strong life till that question "Where is thy brother?" has been answered in the right way. One of the notable scientists of our day, dealing with the human situation, paid a striking tribute to the supremacy and finality of the law of Christ when he said that men must learn the truth of what Christ said, "It is more blessed to give than to receive."

The world's great need today is to take God at His word and accept the biblical and Christian teaching that all men are brothers and that, as Paul said in his address to the philosophers at Mars' Hill, "God . . . hath made of one blood all nations of men for to dwell on the face of the earth." "Who is weak," asks Paul, "and I am not weak? Who is offended, and I burn not?" The famous seventeenth-century preacher and poet John Donne, in his *Devotions*, writes of the ringing of bells—how they toll for the sick and for the dying, and how they speak to the soul of every man. In a celebrated passage he says:

> No man is an island entire of itself. Every man is a piece of continent, a part of the main. If a clod be washed away by the sea, Europe is the less, as well as if a promontory were, as well as if a manor of thy friends or of thine own were. Any man's death diminishes me, because I am involved in mankind. Therefore, never send to know for whom the bell tolls. It tolls for thee.

William Lloyd Garrison, the famous abolitionist and editor of the *Liberator*, was also one of the early advocates of world peace. It was he who wrote the charter for a peace society in

1838. This charter said, "We recognize but one King and Law Giver, one Judge and Ruler of mankind. We love the land of our nativity only as we love all other lands. The interests and rights of American citizens are not dearer to us than those of the whole human race."

Where art thou, then, as to thy brother man? Where art thou as to thine own, that is, those who are united to you by your own flesh and blood? Charles Lamb had a brother who had a lucrative post but omitted entirely his duty to the home. He left the care of the home and the at times mentally deranged sister Mary to the younger brother. When he saw the need of his own family, Charles willingly forwent marriage with a woman for whom he had a deep attachment and became father, mother, brother, son, and husband in that home. He denied himself for his sister and for thirty years watched over her with a tender solicitude. A friend relates how, when one of her periods of insanity was upon her, he would see the brother and sister walking hand in hand across the field to the old asylum, both their faces bathed in tears. A sad story, and yet a grand story of loyalty and affection.

WHERE ART THOU AS TO CHRIST?

When the enemies of Jesus brought Him before the tribunal of Pilate, the Roman procurator said to them, "What shall I do then with Jesus which is called Christ?" He was asking that question of the enemies of Jesus; but in another and deeper sense he was asking the question of his own soul. So God speaks to you. What wilt thou do with Christ? What wilt thou do with the way of life that He teaches? What wilt thou do with His death for sinners on the cross? What wilt thou do with His offer of eternal life? What wilt thou do with His pleading invitation to come unto Him? Other voices speak against Christ and against the verdict of conscience, just as they did that morning in Pilate's judgment court. In Pilate's case the voice of the mob, the voice of the enemies of Christ, prevailed over the still, clear, unmistakable voice of conscience in the breast of Pilate. And their voices, the evangelist says, "prevailed." Whose voice will prevail with you?

Where art thou too as to the cause of Christ in this world? Are you identified with His cause and with His church? At the age of sixteen Theodore Roosevelt presented himself to the minister of the Collegiate Church of St. Nicholas, New York, asking to be allowed to unite with the church, saying, "I would like to become a member of the church. I feel that one who believes as firmly in the Bible and Christianity as I do should say so publicly." Have you done that? Where art thou as to the public confession of Christ? Where art thou as to His work and His cause in this world? Although you bear His name, are you leaving it to others to be His witness, to pray for His cause, to fight for Him?

May this first of all questions, and the greatest of all questions, echo in every breast. And when we hear that voice speaking, "Where art thou?" may we answer it. That question from God brought out two facts: first, that man is lost, that he has hid himself from God; and second, that God comes to seek man. What if God let us wander from Him but did not come to seek for us? What if He let us sin but did not call us to repentance and did not say to us, "How can I let thee go?" What if He made His covenant with us and gave us His commandment and then, when we had broken His commandment, did not come to seek after us and to say to us, "Where art thou?" Wonderful question that is! A question of judgment and condemnation, indeed; but thank God, more than that, a question also that echoes with tender and immeasurable love and compassion and which calls each one of us to return to God.

"Where art thou?" Whatever your answer may be, however it may stand with you tonight, wherever thou art, you can be where and what you ought to be. Christ told of a young man who had wandered far from his father's home and his father's country and had gone farther and farther and deeper and deeper in the ways of sin. But the father's love followed him; and one day in the far country the son heard that same voice that spoke in Eden to Adam speaking to him, "Where art thou?" He realized then where he was, in the far country, in rags, starving, among the swine. But the voice that spake to him saying, "Where art thou?" let him know that this was not where he ought to be, that there was another place that God had reserved for him and which He wanted him to fill. And he said within his heart, "I will arise and go to my father, and will say unto him, Father, I have sinned against heaven, and before thee, and am no more worthy to be called thy son: make me as one of thy hired servants." That is what he said as soon as he heard the voice of God speaking to him, asking, "Where art thou?" And he not only said it, but he did it! He not only said, "I will arise and go to my father," but "he arose, and came to his father." And there was music and dancing, and there was joy among the angels of heaven because a man who had been where he ought not to have been had come back to his true place and to his true home and to his father's house.

2

WILT THOU GO
WITH THIS MAN?

"And they called Rebekah, and said unto her,
Wilt thou go with this man?" (Genesis 24:58)

He had traveled a long distance, a six weeks' journey across the desert, all the way from Hebron to Haran in Mesopotamia, to find out whether she would go or not. But the answer that she gave, taking into consideration who she was, made it a well-spent journey.

Burials and betrothals, births and deaths, sepulchers and marriage altars, how close they come together in life! Abraham had buried Sarah, his wife, in the gloom and shadows of the cave of Machpelah. Then, knowing that it would not be long before his time came to sleep in that same cave, he took up the important business of finding a wife for his son Isaac.

Although he was forty years of age, Isaac was still unmarried. There were probably three reasons for this. First of all, he was a reticent, quiet, bashful sort of young man. Second, a very close and tender relationship had existed between him and his parents as the son of their old age and the child of the promise. And third, the family was living in the land of idolaters, the Canaanites. It might do for his half brother Ishmael, the son of the bond woman, to marry a woman of Egypt, his mother's race and country, but that would never do for Isaac, child of the promise.

Abraham summoned Eliezer, the steward of his household, and exacted of him an oath, that he would not take a wife for Isaac of the daughters of the Canaanites. Then he directed him to go down to Mesopotamia where some of Abraham's relatives, the descendants of his brother Nahor, still lived. When Abraham was migrating from Ur of Chaldees, his father and his brother Nahor had remained behind at Haran, halfway to Canaan, and settled there, while Abraham had pushed on to the Land of Promise. This was the place to which Abraham sent his servant to seek a wife for Isaac.

The old steward said in effect to Abraham, "What if the woman whom I select will not be willing to follow me unto this land? Will it be all right if I bring Isaac down to marry her, or someone else, and live in Haran?" To this Abraham gave the high answer of faith. He told Eliezer that the Lord God of heaven, who had called him out from his father's house and the land of his kindred, would send His angel before him, and he would be guided to the right woman for Isaac. But whatever happened, Isaac was not to go down to Mesopotamia to live. Wife or no wife, that was not to be. Abraham and his family had been called out of that land; and in God's plan there are no backward steps.

With ten camels laden with goods and presents and a considerable retinue, as befitted so great a chief of the desert as Abraham, Eliezer bade Abraham farewell and set out for the far-distant city of Nahor, or Haran. On their way they went, the caravan of camels with their noiseless tread and their rhythmic, swinging gait. Even today a caravan of camels in the Eastern lands, their bodies silhouetted against the endless horizon, is the most picturesque sight on the desert or on all the roads of the East.

At length the caravan drew nigh to the city of Nahor. It was eventide when they arrived at the well outside the city. If you were to take out of the Bible the stories of the different wells, it would be a much poorer book. At this well of Haran we have the beginning of the romance of Isaac and Rebekah. At another well in this same Mesopotamian country, indeed, as far as we can tell, the same well, Rachel was watering her flocks when fugitive Jacob arrived and drew water for her and fell in love with her at first sight. It was for water out of the well by the gate at Bethlehem that David longed for a drink when he cried out in his hiding place and stronghold, "Oh, that one would give me drink of the water of the well of Bethlehem, which is by the gate!" And that, I have always felt, was far more than just a desire to drink of the water out of that well. I feel sure that it was an expression of that thirst which rises from the soul, a thirst and a longing for the happiness and peace and innocence of his youth. It was by the well in the wilderness that Hagar, cast out and despairing, nourished and restored the dying Ishmael. And it was at another well in the wilderness that the same Hagar learned God's care for her and called it "The Well of Him that Liveth and Seeth Me." It was by the well of Jacob that Jesus, weary and thirsty, sat one day when the woman of Samaria came to draw water. How often, traveling through those lands, I have sat down on the curb of those ancient wells, watched the people from the village coming and going, refreshed myself with its cool water, and in imagination have seen Jacob kiss Rachel, Rebekah draw water for the camels of Eliezer, heard David's cry for water out of the well of Bethlehem by the gate or the accents of Hagar's glad surprise, "Thou, God, seest me!" and listened again to our Lord as he talked with that five-times-married, sinful, and hopeless woman at the well of Samaria.

The eventide is the time when the womenfolk come out to the well to draw water. Even today in the southern countries of Europe, Italy, Greece, and Spain, you can still see the women coming out with their earthen vessels, carried as a rule on the top of their heads, women with motionless shoulders walking along with singular grace and dignity. So it was that Eliezer on this evening saw the women coming to that ancient well at Haran. As the thirsty camels put down their heads to drink, Eliezer made his prayer to God, asking for a sign. The sign is to be that he will say to one of the women, "Let down thy pitcher, I pray thee, that I may drink"; and she was to answer, "Drink, and I will give thy camels to drink also." Eliezer himself was to select the young woman whom he would so address, and then the fulfillment of the matter was in the hands of God. The young woman who so responded to Eliezer was to be regarded as God's choice for the wife of Isaac.

Among those coming to the well, her vessel poised gracefully upon her shoulder, was the beautiful daughter of Bethuel, Rebekah. "And the damsel was very fair to look upon." Eliezer could see that at once and perhaps felt, even without the sign which followed, that she would make a good wife for Isaac. Then, according to his covenant with God, he said to Rebekah, "Let me, I pray thee, drink a little water of thy pitcher," and with gracious mien Rebekah answered, "Drink, my lord," and, letting down her pitcher which she had filled at the well, gave him to drink. When Eliezer had quenched his own thirst, she said, "I will draw water for thy camels also." And then, without waiting for an answer, emptied her pitcher into the trough, and going back and forth to the well kept filling the trough for the thirsty camels. The camel is a strange animal. He can travel for many days without drinking, but when he does drink, he makes up for the long time between the drinks. Once on the Egnatian highway, near Philippi, I saw the camels of a caravan drinking at one of these old wells. What a prodigious amount of water they were able to put down! And so it was here. But Rebekah, as quick and agile as she was lissome and beautiful, kept running down the steps to the well, drawing the vessel up from the dark, cool depths below, filling her pitcher, and emptying it again into the troughs until the camels had quenched their thirst.

The old steward took out of his pack the golden earrings and golden bracelets and presented them to the beautiful girl. Then he asked her whose daughter she was and if he could lodge in her father's house. Rebekah told him who she was, the daughter of Bethuel, the son of Abraham's brother, and thus the great-niece of Abraham. This she followed up with a cordial invitation to Eliezer and his company to come in and lodge at their home. Now the old man was sure that this was the woman, and, lifting up his head, he offered his prayer of thanksgiving, "Blessed be the Lord God of my master Abraham, who hath not left destitute my master of his mercy and his truth. I being in the way, the Lord led me to the house of my master's brethren."

When Rebekah had run to her home and had told her

brother Laban, not yet the churlish Laban, the father of Rachel and who cheated Jacob, he gave Eliezer a cordial invitation to come in and stay with the family. They put up the camels and fed them and gave water for Eliezer and his men to wash their feet and then set meat before them. But Eliezer would not eat till he had stated his errand. He related the commission that Abraham had given him, to seek a wife for Isaac; how he had asked God for a sign at the well; how Rebekah had come out with her pitcher on her shoulder and had courteously granted his request and had drawn water both for him and for his camels; and how now he felt sure that she was the one chosen of God to be the wife of Isaac. When they heard all this, Rebekah's father Bethuel and her brother Laban confessed together, "The thing proceedeth from the Lord."

The next morning Eliezer asked permission to depart and to take Rebekah with him to his master, Isaac. The father and the brother suggested a stay and delay for a few days, at least ten. But Eliezer would not agree to this. Then they said, "We will call the damsel, and enquire at her mouth." So they brought her in and said to her, "Wilt thou go with this man?" Without a moment's hesitation, Rebekah answered, "I will go." She was then mounted on one of the camels and, accompanied by her faithful nurse Deborah, set out on the long journey to Hebron and to Isaac. As they rode away, her father and brother and mother blessed her and said to her, "Be thou the mother of thousands of millions, and let thy seed possess the gate of those which hate them." And that is a prophecy which was fulfilled, for through her descendants Rebekah became the mother of thousands of millions.

Now we come to the end of this beautiful idyl. Here we have the wedding march, not as in Lohengrin, but the wedding march of the camels. The weary journey of six weeks drew to an end. Near another well, that very well where God had spoken to outcast and despairing Hagar, Isaac was meditating at the eventide in the field, when he lifted up his eyes "and behold the camels were coming." Just at the same moment Rebekah lifted up her eyes and saw for the first time the form of her husband, for whom she had said, "I will go." "And Isaac brought her into his mother Sarah's tent, . . . and she became his wife; and he loved her: and Isaac was comforted after his mother's death."

THE QUESTION STILL ASKED AND ANSWERED

"Wilt thou go with this man?" they asked. And Rebekah answered, "I will go." And still that question is asked, and still the woman answers, "I will go." Rebekah said, "I will go," although it meant leaving her father's house and never beholding again the faces of her father or mother or brother or maiden friends at the well of Haran. She said, "I will go," although it meant the long month and a half journey on the back of the camel over the burning sands of the desert. She said, "I will go," although it meant going to the land of the Canaanites to dwell among a strange people.

That answer of Rebekah has never been wanting. The echo of it has never died away. "I will go," the woman has said, although it meant leaving home and kindred. "I will go," although it meant a long, terrible steerage passage in a sailing vessel across the stormy Atlantic from some port in Sweden or Germany or France or Scotland or England or Ireland to the shores of an unknown land. "I will go," the woman has said, although it meant leaving her home in Australia or in Britain and crossing the thousands of miles of ocean to join her soldier-lover in the New World. "I will go," the woman has said, although it meant sitting for weeks and months under the canopy of the prairie schooner, behind the plodding oxen, through the rivers and across the plains and over the mountains to California's shores. "I will go," although it meant giving up a home of refinement and luxury for a cabin in the wilderness or a one-room, back-story apartment. I knew a woman who said to a young theological student from the United States, "I will go." She left her father's house, the mansion with its gardens and conservatories, servants and the coachmen and the refinements of the city, for the long journey across the ocean to the tiny hamlet on the western Ohio plain where her husband's modest frame church stood. Yet she went, and, despite many trials and tribulations, remained. "I will go!" By the music of that response the world still marches on!

The story of how Abraham's old servant sought God's guidance and asked for a sign which God granted him is one that applies not only to a search for a wife, but to all the experiences of life. When he realized how God had led him, he said, "I being in the way, the Lord led me." He asked for God's guidance. He put himself in the way of it, and that guidance was granted him. That is the thing to do in all the affairs of your life. "In all thy ways acknowledge him, and he shall direct thy paths." "Commit thy way unto the Lord; trust also in him; and he shall bring it to pass." The "angel" which Abraham told his steward would guide him, will guide you too.

But this is an example of guidance and divine Providence in the particular matter of marriage, the relationship between the young man and the young woman. There was one thing that Abraham was decided upon: whatever happened, whether he lived the rest of his days wifeless or not, Isaac must not marry an idolater, an unbeliever. That was not to be thought of. The same principle is a good rule for young men and young women to follow today. The mixed marriage between the Christian and Jew, between Protestant and Roman Catholic, between the Christian and the pagan is fraught with peril and is a dangerous course to take. In the ardor of early affection young people may think that they can overcome by mutual common sense and affection difficulties that arise in such a marriage. But experience lifts its voice against such an expectation. I have seen circumstances arise out of marriages such as this, where Solomon himself would not have had the wisdom to solve the difficulties. Particularly dangerous and fraught with unhappiness is the marriage of a Christian with an unbeliever. So the apostle said to the men and women of Corinth, "Be ye not unequally yoked together with unbelievers. . . . What part hath he that believeth with an infidel?" If one has real Christian faith and adores Christ as the Son of God and the Redeemer of his soul, then between such a person and an unbelieving partner there is a fixed gulf. The ideal condition, where the husband will delight to love his wife, even as Christ loved the church and gave himself for it, will be the marriage between two persons who both love the Lord and hold in common the highest things.

Grant's favorite general, James Birdseye McPherson, and

Sherman's also, who fell untimely in the battle of Atlanta in 1864, just before he was to receive a furlough so that he could go to Baltimore and be married to the woman of his choice, had written of his fiancée to his mother. In the letter he wrote he told his mother that she was "intelligent, refined, generous-hearted, and a Christian. This will suit you as it does me, for it lies at the foundation of every pure and elevated character." Those four qualifications which McPherson observed in his fiancée are worthy of the thoughtful consideration of every young man who is ready to ask a young woman, "Wilt thou go?" and of every young woman who is ready to answer, "I will go." Here are the four things General McPherson mentioned: intelligence, refinement, a generous heart, and Christian faith.

The newspapers abound in the stories of unhappiness and unfaithfulness in marriage, and the ghastly statistics of the divorce courts today are indeed staggering. But we must not forget the thousands upon thousands of marriages which in reality are "until death do us part." These marriages do not get into the newspapers. They are not featured in the smart-set magazines. But they are the marriages which build the homes of the nation. They are the marriages which are the fountain source whence flow the streams of happiness and of blessing. They are the marriages of which it may be said:

> Then blend they—like green leaves with golden flowers,
>   Into one beautiful and perfect whole
> And life's long night is ended, and the way
>   Lies open onward to eternal day.
>
>   —Edwin Arnold, "Destiny"

3

WHAT IF HE GAIN THE WORLD AND LOSE HIS SOUL?

"For what is a man profited, if he shall gain the whole world, and lose his own soul?" (Matthew 16:26)

In what a competent judge has said is the greatest passage in French prose, Pascal wrote:

> Man is but a reed, the feeblest thing in nature. But he is a reed that thinks. It needs not that the universe arise to crush him. An exhalation, a drop of water suffices to destroy him; but were the universe to crush man, man is yet nobler than the universe, for he knows that he dies, and the universe, even in prevailing against him, knows not its power.

It is about that thing in man which is greater than the universe in which man lives that we shall consider. There are three things that I shall say on this subject. First, that man has or is a living and immortal soul; second, that the soul has suffered injury and damage; and third, that Christ discovers, redeems, and restores the soul of man.

MAN IS A LIVING SOUL

What do we mean by the soul? I shall not draw fine-spun

definitions or darken words without knowledge, but I shall take the plain biblical thought of the soul as man's moral, spiritual, and never-dying part. There is no doubt that is what Christ meant when He used the word "soul." In Mark the question of Christ reads: "What shall it profit a man, if he shall gain the whole world, and lose his own soul?" In Matthew it runs: "What is a man profited, if he shall gain the whole world, and lose his own soul?" But in Luke it reads: "For what is a man advantaged, if he gain the whole world, and lose himself?" The soul is thyself, myself. It is that in man which loves, hopes, prays, believes, aspires, is tempted, sins, repents, and can be eternally saved.

Subjected to every test, the soul is the supreme thing in man. There is the test of subtraction. That is, take a man's soul from him and add the world to him and what have you left? Nothing but an animal, nothing but a clod. But with a soul—"What a piece of work is a man! How noble in reason! How infinite in faculty! In form and moving how express and admirable! In action how like an angel! In apprehension how like a god!"

Another test of the soul's greatness is the purpose of life. Why are we here? What is the meaning of existence? When the first runner, Ahimaaz, came out of the wood where the battle had been fought and where Absalom had fallen, but he himself did not know what had happened, and the anxious King David, waiting at the tower, said to him, "Is the young man Absalom safe?" all the runner could say was, "I saw a great tumult, but I knew not what it was." Is that all there is to life? Just a great and meaningless tumult in the thicket of existence? Just a noise, full of sound and fury, signifying nothing? If life is for knowledge, for fame, for pleasure, for glory, then it is a grim, sardonic joke. But if life is a trial, a probation, if the purpose of it is the production of moral and spiritual qualities and their development here in this life and their coronation in the life which is to come, then life is just the stuff to try our souls on. But without the soul, life is nothing but a tumult.

Another test of the greatness of the soul is that of endurance, permanence. Over the three doors of beautiful Milan Cathedral are three symbols and three inscriptions. Over the door on the left are roses, with the words, "That which pleases is but for a moment." Over the door on the right are thorns, with the words, "That which troubles is but for a moment." But over the central door is a cross with the inscription, "That alone is important which endures forever." The soul is the important part of man because it endures forever.

A thousand empires rise,
A thousand empires fall,
But still the eternal stars
Shine over all.

At length the stars themselves
Into the night are thrust;
And suns and systems pale,
Go down in dust.

But let the universe itself
Back into darkness roll;
Two lights death cannot quench—
God and the Soul.

—Author Unknown

The highest test of the value of any object is what has been done for it. And how great a thing was done for the soul of man, so great that when it was done and the Son of God died for the soul's redemption, the earth rocked and the sun hid his face in amazement! That is the supreme appraisal of the value of man's soul—the death of Christ for it upon the cross.

Such, then, is the soul of man. It alone explains man. You may stand your skeletons, from the highest anthropoid ape up to man, against the walls of the museum and you may put your jars of germs upon the shelves of the laboratory, but you have not explained man. You have not explained the tears of compassion, the flame of righteous indignation, the hope of the hereafter, the ambitions of a commencement season, a sonnet of Shakespeare or Milton or the Twenty-third Psalm. Over the great Hall of Man at the New York World's Fair were these words of Augustine: "Man wonders o'er the restless sea, the sight of sky, the flowing waters, and forget that of all wonders man himself is the most wonderful."

Today this most wonderful thing in man, the soul, suffers eclipse. The soul is the real forgotten man. It is forgotten in education. What honor is done to the soul, what place given to it in our colleges and universities? The soul is forgotten in enterprises and reforms to save society, for those schemes would clothe and feed man and give him a comfortable place in the universe but neglect his soul. Even in the church the soul is sometimes forgotten, for a large part of the church seems to have found something more important to do than to save man's soul and is instead engaged in the highest enterprise of society. Yet it is a striking fact that the church has ever had the greatest influence upon society when it devoted its energies to the salvation of man's soul.

All that is summed up in a striking way by Chauncey Brewster Tinker, professor of English at Yale, who said:

> The disease of the world today is the loss of faith in the moral nature of man. Instead of thinking of the august character and destiny of man, we have been preoccupied with him as one of the highest order of primates. Man has been found to be a speaking animal. The view that he is also a son of God is an amiable but deluded notion of our ill-formed ancestors.

On the Amazon River there is said to be a tribe of Indians who, at certain seasons of the year, squat on the ground and refuse to move, saying that they are waiting for their souls to catch up with their bodies. That is indeed the great need of the world today. It should sit down for a little and let the soul catch up with the body.

THE SOUL HAS SUFFERED DISASTER AND INJURY

This is the Christian doctrine of the fall of man, of all the Christian doctrines the most ridiculed and discounted, and yet of all the doctrines the one which is most confirmed by history and experience. As Bernard Shaw put it in *Back to Methuselah:* "Where is the fall? You might as well take me to the foot of

Snowden and say to me, 'Where is the mountain?'" Yes, the fall is everywhere. We do not hear often today that once popular and flippant remark, that the only way man falls is upward. Man's faith in a law of inevitable and invincible development of progress, regardless of what men and nations do or are, has been rudely shaken by world events. If that is all, then all we have to expect is the perpetual recurrence of what now is. If the only thing we can count upon is this supposed universal and inevitable law of progress, then woe to mankind.

Something has happened to man's soul to dislocate his life, to destroy the beautiful harmony of the soul with himself, and that something is sin—as eternal as human history, as universal as human nature. It is this alone which accounts for what we see in the world today, for the discord of man's life, for the fact that his heart is a fountain whence flow both sweet and bitter waters. It is this which accounts for that civil war in the breast of man which Paul discovered in his great experience in moral psychology when he found two men at war with one another within his breast, the law of the flesh and the law of the mind. It is this disaster, sin, that accounts for the long-resounding chord of human woe and sorrow. It is this that explains how it is that man is at once a cloaca (sewer) and a temple, the glory and the shame of the universe.

Some years ago in Charleston, South Carolina, I came across the sermon of a seer-minded and prophetic preacher. This was the burden of the sermon: When the man and the woman were driven out of Eden and lay down under a tree to sleep, the Spirits of the Air and the Earth and the Waters and the Fire came and stole away man's soul. Then they fell into a dispute as to what they should do with it. Each one claimed it, and unable to secure it, all agreed that they would hide man's soul.

But where could they hide it so that man could never find it again? The Spirit of the Earth said, "Hide the soul of man deep within me, so deep down in the earth that he will never find it." But the Spirit of the Water said, "No, man will invent some secret and mysterious power by which he can tell what is under the earth, and he will find his soul again. Do not hide the soul of man in the earth, but hide it in me. Hide it ten thousand fathoms down in the deepest and darkest waters of the sea. There man will never find his soul."

But the Spirit of the Air said, "No, do not hide the soul of man in the sea. Man will invent a ship which will sail under the sea, and he will search for his soul and find it, even in the deepest and coldest and darkest waters of the ocean. Do not hide the soul of man in the sea. Hide it in me. Hide it up high in the highest heavens, clear beyond the remotest star. There man will never find his soul."

But the Spirit of Fire said, "No, do not hide the soul of man in the heavens. Do not hide it among the remotest stars, for with his wonderful mind man will invent some ship of the air by which he will ascend to the highest heavens, and there he will search for his soul until he finds it. No, do not hide the soul of man in the heavens, but hide the soul of man in me. In my white and consuming flames man will never find his soul."

So they hid the soul of man in the Spirit of Fire, within the flame. But lo, when they put the soul of man into the fire, it came out with a new and more wonderful beauty and clearness than ever before!

Perplexed and in despair as to what to do and where to put man's soul so that he could never find it, the four Spirits returned to their master, the Devil, and asked him what they should do. When he heard of what they had planned, Satan laughed and said, "Fools! I will tell you what to do. I will tell you where to hide man's soul so that he will never find it. Hide it in man!" Yes, that is the tragedy of man's life! His soul is hid within himself!

CHRIST DISCOVERS, REDEEMS, AND RESTORES THE SOUL OF MAN

It was the tragedy of sin, the loss of man's soul, that brought Christ to earth. This is the fact that lies back of the sublime transaction of Calvary. Christ asked two questions about the soul. They are often erroneously thought of as the same, but how different they are! The first question was this: "What shall it profit a man, if he shall gain the whole world, and lose his own soul?" That question is not difficult to answer. Every man, whether he acts on the truth of it or not, knows that that would be a sad and wretched bargain. But the other question is quite different: "What shall a man give in exchange for his soul?" Christ, you see, did not say, "What shall a man *take* for his soul?" He knew how little men will take for their soul. You and I know how little, alas, how little, men will take for their souls. A fading honor, a few dollars, a moment's comfort, a kiss and an embrace, even so small a thing as that, men will take for their souls. But Christ did not ask that. What he asked was this: "What shall a man *give* for his soul?" After he has scarred his soul with sin, after he has sold his soul and betrayed himself, what can he give to get his soul back? Answer that, ye who sit in the seats of the mighty! Answer that, if you can, scholars and scientists of our universities! Answer that, dictators and despots of the world! No, you cannot answer it. No man is great or wise enough to answer it. Only the Poet of Calvary could answer it. Christ alone can give that which will get a man back his soul. There upon the cross he paid the sublime, mysterious, awful, transcendent, overwhelming price of the soul's redemption.

Here is a man who comes to God to get back his soul. First he brings his tears: "Here are my tears, as pure as crystal, like the tears of Peter when he went out into the night and wept bitterly. Give me back my soul in exchange." When that does not avail, he brings his repentance: "Here is my repentance, as sincere as the repentance of the dying thief, to whom Jesus opened the gates of paradise. Give me back my soul." When that does not avail, he comes with his remorse and says: "Here is my remorse, as sharp and bitter as that of Judas. Give me back my soul." When that does not avail, he comes with his prayers: "Here are my prayers, as earnest as those of David, when he besought God not to cast him away from his presence or to take his Holy Spirit from him." But this does not avail. Then I saw one come before God with a vial in his hand, and he who sat upon the throne said to him, "What hast thou there?" And he answered, "One drop of the blood of Christ shed for sinners upon the cross." And all the angels shouted as the King upon His throne said, "Give him back his soul!"

Potentially every man is a redeemed soul, just as historically he is a created soul. Live, then, as a redeemed soul. Outside of the Bible there is perhaps no passage more noble in its melodious prose, or more to be commended to young men and young women, than that glorious passage where John Milton gives the reason why he was kept from the gross transgressions which marred the lives of his fellow students at Cambridge. He gives two reasons why a man ought not to sin against God and himself. The first is the dignity of God's image upon him by creation. The second is the price of his redemption, visibly marked upon his forehead. "He thinks himself both a fit person to do the noblest and goodliest deeds, and much better worth than to debase and defile, with such a debasement and pollution as sin is, himself, so highly ransomed and ennobled to a new friendship and filial relation with God."

You have been highly ransomed and ennobled to a new friendship with God. Live worthy of that high calling! When Christ asked those questions about the soul, He was not warning us against temptations which do not exist. Still as of old Satan desires to have you that he may sift you as wheat, that he may sift the soul out of you. The best, therefore, that I can do is to commend you to the Creator, Redeemer, and Preserver of your souls, to Him who paid the price of your redemption on the cross, our Lord Jesus Christ. Choose Him today. Commence with Him now. Then this will be a commencement day and season, not in academic and class association, but in deep religious and spiritual reality, a commencement that shall know no ending, a companionship which shall grow in power and joy from day to day, and the glory and beauty of which it will take the unending ages of eternity to declare and reveal.

4

WHAT SHALL I DO WITH JESUS?

"Pilate saith unto them, What shall I do then with Jesus?" (Matthew 27:22)

Pilate asked that of the scribes and Pharisees and the chief priests and the crowds whose coarse clamor had awakened him on that early Friday morning. But in reality he asked the question of himself, "What shall I do then with Jesus?"

I have been looking recently at Munkacsy's famous painting "Christ Before Pilate." I saw it first some thirty years ago, when it was purchased by John Wanamaker and brought to this country and put on exhibition at his Philadelphia store. A helmeted Roman soldier, with his spear held in a horizontal position, is keeping back the crowd. In this crowd you can see a fanatic, his two arms flung aloft and his mouth wide open, as he shouts, "Crucify Him! Crucify Him!" Another man, lifted up on the shoulders of others in the crowd, points his hand at Jesus and appeals to Pilate for a verdict. In the crowd there is just one friendly face and that is the face of a young mother with a sweet babe in her arms as they look down on Jesus. One fellow is leaning over a barrier and looking around into the face of Jesus with a scornful smile upon his countenance. On either side of Jesus are the scribes and Pharisees, and the high priest Caiaphas is standing on the steps of the judgment seat looking toward Pilate but pointing toward Jesus, making an accusation to the governor against Him and demanding His death. On a bench to the left of the judgment seat sits a corpulent banker, robed in white and with his face turned toward Jesus in a hostile and scornful glance. Clad in a white seamless garment, and with His hands bound in front of Him, Jesus stands just at the end of the soldier's javelin, looking toward Pilate. The procurator sits at the head of the steps of the judgment seat under a marble arch, his white robe lined with purple. The face is strong and intelligent, but upon it there is the deep cast of perplexity and uncertainty as he looks out, not at Jesus, not at Caiaphas, not at the scribes and Pharisees, not at the shouting mob, but with unfocused eye, as if searching the depths of his own mind and heart. His perplexity is betrayed by the way he is holding his hands in front of him. One hand is laid upon the other, and the fingers of the left hand are lifted, the way men do when they are pondering some matter and trying to come to a decision.

THE SUDDEN CRISIS

How suddenly the great crises of life strike! If I could tell you that tomorrow night at twelve o'clock you would be subjected to some dangerous temptation, or that a month from today you would be called upon to pass through the trial of some great sorrow or sickness, you could, in a way, prepare yourself and fortify yourself against such a temptation and trial. But that is not the way those hours come in life. They come unannounced. The crises of the soul break suddenly upon us. So it was here. Little could Pilate have imagined, as he lay down to sleep on that Thursday night, that the next day was to be the crisis of his life. Little could he have foreseen, when he was aroused on that Friday morning by his officers who told him that the Jews had brought a prisoner and were demanding his immediate trial, or when, angry and impatient at the turbulent Jews, he took his place upon the judgment seat, that this unknown prisoner was going to try his soul and search his heart. But so it came to pass.

You can see Pilate seated there on the judgment throne which stood just outside the palace. It had two names, one the "Gabatha," meaning "an elevated place," because the Roman law required that the accused must stand on a place where he could see and where others could see him. The other name was the "Pavement," because the ground was paved with a mosaic of richly colored stones. Leading up to the judgment seat of Pilate were white marble steps. On either side of the governor's chair, and cut into the marble of the archway under which it stood, were the familiar letters which one could read all over the Roman world at that time: S.P.Q.R.—The Roman Senate and People.

When Pilate took his seat, he looked out over the assembled crowd and the high priests, the scribes, and the Pharisees, with a glance of scorn and contempt, as if saying to himself, "Miserable, execrable Jews! Now what trouble are you stirring up!" Then he called out, "Bring up the prisoner!" The guards of the Sanhedrin led Jesus before the judgment seat. I wish I had been there to note the look upon Pilate's face when his eye first fell on Jesus. Immediately the glance of contempt and scorn which he had flashed upon the Pharisees and the priests and the crowd disappeared. The harsh, cruel look faded from his face as he looked upon Jesus. That one look at Jesus precipitated the battle in Pilate's soul. Here was a man who had a bad record. He had not scrupled to mingle the blood of the Galileans with the blood of the sacrifices they brought to the Temple. Why should he be troubled when he beheld Jesus? Why should the question of putting Him to death have perplexed Pilate, who had put so many men to death without the slightest compuction of conscience? Yet the moment he looked upon Jesus, the voice of conscience began to speak in Pilate's heart. The better man that lies within all men, sleeping but not dead, was awakened. Pilate knew that the Man before him was innocent. Perhaps he said to himself at the very beginning, "He is not only an innocent man, but may be more than a man."

THE TRUCE OF GOD

Whittier has a verse in which he speaks of those special moments of grace which God gives to the soul. He calls such a moment the "truce of God." Peter had such a moment when he cursed his Master in the courtyard of the high priest, and Jesus turned and looked upon him. Judas had such a moment, a truce of God granted him, when Jesus that night at the Lord's Supper washed his feet, with those of the other disciples, and later said to him, "That thou doest, do quickly." Herod Antipas had such a moment, such a truce of God, when his soul was "sorry" when he heard Salome's request for John the Baptist's head. So, called upon to condemn Jesus to be crucified, when Pilate first looked upon Jesus he had, as it were, a truce of God granted to him. By the truce of God I mean a special appeal to turn away from sin and to choose God and righteousness before it is too late and the final decision is made. God may be granting that blessed truce at this very moment to some soul who is tempted to take the wrong path or to turn away from Christ and condemn Him again to be crucified.

Let us see now what use Pilate made of that truce. He must have realized, indeed, that it was the truce of God, for he struggled hard to hold himself back from committing the great iniquity of sentencing Jesus to death. First of all, he told the Jews to take Him and try Him themselves. But they reminded him that it was not lawful for them, under the Roman law, to put anyone to death. That must have stirred Pilate all the more, because it let him know the seriousness of the case. It let him know that these angry, jealous, shouting ecclesiastics and their followers were bent on nothing less than the death of Jesus.

Pilate then took Jesus apart into his chambers in the palace for that memorable interview in which he asked Jesus about the accusation which had been brought against Him, that He claimed to be the King of the Jews, "Art thou the King of the Jews?" Jesus replied, "Sayest thou this thing of thyself, or did others tell it thee of me?" With a touch of scorn in his voice, Pilate answered, "Am I a Jew?" As if he had said, "Do you suppose that I hold conversations and discussions with these miserable Jews over their religion or over those who claim to be their king? Your own people have brought You here. Tell me what You have done." Jesus answered, "My kingdom is not of this world: if my kingdom were of this world, then would my servants fight." Again Jesus had spoken of His kingdom, and Pilate, perplexed and half in doubt, perhaps half in irony, said, "Art thou a king then?" Jesus replied, "To this end was I born, and for this cause came I into the world, that I should bear witness unto the truth." At that Pilate rose from his chair, and walking up and down in his chambers, exclaimed, "What is truth?" I doubt if Bacon was correct when, in his famous essay "Of Truth," he commenced by saying "'What is truth?' said jesting Pilate; and would not stay for an answer."

No, I do not feel that Pilate was jesting when he said that to Jesus. It was perhaps more of a soliloquy than a question put to Jesus. Pilate had listened to the Roman and Greek philosophers discussing truth. During his years as the favorite of the Emperor Claudius, and during his term of office as the procurator of Judea, Pilate had dealt only with hard, practical matters of administration or with sensual and temporal enjoyments. And yet now, in the presence of Jesus, his soul asks itself, "What is truth?" And there was the Truth Himself standing bound before him! I wonder if Pilate had an intimation of that?

Not waiting for his own answer to the question "What is truth?" or for the answer of Jesus, Pilate brought Jesus out to the judgment seat again and said to the crowd that stood around, "I find no fault in him." But the words were no more out of his mouth than a fierce cry went up, "Crucify him, crucify him!" As Pilate stood listening, irritated, perplexed, and somewhat amazed, no doubt, at the bitter hostility of the mob, he heard one loud voice shout, "He stirreth up the people, teaching throughout all Jewry, beginning from Galilee to this place." When he heard that Jesus came from Galilee, it gave Pilate an idea. "Galilee!" he said in effect. "If he comes from Galilee, then I can turn him over to the jurisdiction of Herod, who is king over that region." With that he sent him off to Herod and by so doing hoped to kill two birds with one stone—free himself of responsibility concerning the prisoner and also make friends with Herod, for Herod and Pilate had had a quarrel.

Herod was glad when he saw Jesus, for he had heard much about Him, and he wanted to ask Him many questions. But Jesus answered him not a word. It was this same Herod who had beheaded John the Baptist against the verdict of his own conscience. That was Herod's opportunity, his truce of God, when the Holy Spirit, speaking through his conscience, told him that John was a righteous man and that he ought not to put him to death. He had let that opportunity pass. Now his day of grace was passed. Jesus answered him not a word. Unable to get anything out of Jesus, Herod, to mock Him and His kingly claims, put a scarlet robe on Him and sent Him back to Pilate.

Once again Pilate had to take his place on the judgment seat. Once again this strange, meek, silent, but soul-searching prisoner stood before him. It was just at that moment that Pilate received a message from his wife saying, "Have thou nothing to do with that just man: for I have suffered many things this day in a dream because of him." What was it that Pilate's wife had suffered? What was her agony? Was it a knowledge of the guilt and woe which would forever rest upon Pilate if he gave Christ over to be crucified? Whatever it was, the warning of that dream was to Pilate another gracious truce of God, calling him back from the evil that he did not want to do, but toward which all the circumstances drew him, as a maelstrom sucks a ship down into its deathly embrace.

Then Pilate had another idea. It was the custom at this time of the year for the governor to make a gesture of friendship for the people by pardoning some criminal in prison. "Why not select Jesus?" Pilate said to himself. Calling out to the crowd, he said, "Ye have a custom, that I should release unto you one at the Passover: will ye therefore that I release unto you the King of the Jews?" But the people shouted, "Release unto us Barabbas." Barabbas was in prison, a charge of insurrection and murder against him. They cried against Jesus, "Crucify him, crucify him!"

THE SURRENDER

Once again Pilate had been baffled in his efforts to release Jesus. But Pilate was *determined to let Him go*. He made one more effort. Turning to the centurion, he told him to take the prisoner and scourge Him. When Jesus had been brought back again to the judgment seat after the brutal Roman scourging, the blood pouring from His wounds and staining the mosaic of the pavement, Pilate said, "Behold the man!" It was his hope that this cruel and brutal scourging would be accepted by the Jews as sufficient punishment upon Jesus. But they were not to be thrown off the trail so easily. Inflamed all the more by this sight of His blood, they cried out, "Crucify him, crucify him!" But still Pilate hesitated. Not yet was the battle lost. Still there gleamed for Pilate's soul one single, beautiful ray of God's blessed truce. While he hesitated, he heard a loud, coarse voice in the back of the crowd, "If thou let this man go, thou art not Ceasar's friend." And that was the end of that long hard battle that Pilate had fought to do the right thing. He trembled at the thought of having the people accuse him as an enemy to Ceasar, and that particular Ceasar, Tiberius, the brutal misanthrope of Capri. Calling for a basin of water, Pilate washed his hands, according to the old ritual, saying, "I am innocent of the blood of this just person. See ye to it." He then released Jesus to be crucified.

That was what Pilate did with Jesus. He was not the first or the last man to wash in that basin. What a drama that is! Pilate, struggling for his soul—his reason, his judgment, his fears, his superstition, all telling him what to do with Jesus—and yet, in spite of that, condemning Him to be crucified.

THE QUESTION ECHOES TODAY

Pilate's question still echoes today. What will you do with Jesus? What have you done with Him? You cannot ignore Him. Pilate tried to do that. He tried to shift responsibility, first to the Jews, when he asked them to try Him, and second, to Herod, when he sent Him off to him. But in the end Pilate himself had to make the decision. You are the man! You must decide!

What will you do with Jesus? Some oppose Him and persecute Him. That is what Saul of Tarsus did until his eyes were opened that day by the Gates of Damascus when the bright light shone from heaven and Paul heard a voice saying, "Saul, Saul, why persecutest thou me?" Paul did not realize before that time that in opposing the church and the Christians he was persecuting Jesus. He thought that Jesus was an imposter who was in a well-deserved criminal's grave. But then he learned that he was persecuting Christ. What is the attitude of your heart toward Christ? Have you been opposing Him, resisting

Him, and so persecuting Him? If so, would that you might hear the voice that Paul heard, "Why persecutest thou me?"

I would like to ask this question too of Christians, as well as of unbelievers: What will you do with Jesus? What are you doing for Him? Is your life a credit to Him? Does your life adorn His Gospel? Is the church any stronger or purer because you are in it? Is the cause of Christ advanced in the world because of your efforts or prayers or sacrifices?

But most of all, this is a question for those outside the church, for anyone who has not yet come to Christ, "What will you do with Jesus?" On Sunday night, October 8, 1871, Dwight L. Moody was preaching to a great congregation in Farwell Hall, Chicago. This was the text of his sermon: "What shall I do then with Jesus?" At the close of the sermon he said, "I wish you would take this text home with you and turn it over in your minds during the week, and next Sabbath we will come to Calvary and the cross, and we will decide what to do with Jesus of Nazareth." Then, as usual, he turned to Sankey and asked him to sing a hymn. Sankey sang:

> Today, the Savior calls,
>   For refuge fly;
> The storm of justice falls,
>   And death is nigh.

But the hymn was never finished; for while Sankey was singing, there was the rush and roar of fire engines on the street outside, and the heavens were crimson with the reflection of the great Chicago fire. In the morning Chicago lay in ashes. To his dying day Moody was full of regret because he had told that congregation to wait until next Sabbath to decide what to do with Jesus. "I have never dared," he said, "to give an audience a week to think of their salvation since. If they were lost, they might rise up in judgment against me. I have never seen that congregation since. I will never meet those people until I meet them in another world. But I want to tell of one lesson I learned that night which I have never forgotten; and that is when I preach, to press Christ upon the people then and there and try to bring them to a decision on the spot. I would rather have that right hand cut off than to give an audience a week now to decide what to do with Jesus."

Remembering that incident in Moody's life and preaching, certainly I will not ask you to wait until next Sabbath or wait until tomorrow or to wait until the next hour to decide what you will do with Christ. I ask you to answer the question and to answer it now. And because of the answer that you give, may you look back to this hour, through all the years of your life and through the unending years of eternity, as the great and blessed and happy hour of your life, because then, when the question was asked you, "What will I do with Jesus?" you answered, "I will take Him as my King, my Friend, and my Redeemer."

5

WHAT MUST I DO TO BE SAVED?

"And suddenly there was a great earthquake. . . . And the
keeper of the prison . . . fell down before Paul and Silas . . .
and said, Sirs, what must I do to be saved?" (Acts 16:26–30)

Good men who were prisoners sometimes conferred great
benefits on their jailers. We need but mention John Brown
and John Bunyan among others. But never did a prisoner con-
fer so great a benefit on his jailer as Paul did on the jailer of
Philippi. When Jesus sent the devils out of the man of Gadara
into the swine, the owners of the swine besought Jesus to
depart out of their coasts. The fall in the pork market meant
more to them than the redemption of a lost and devil-possessed
man. This same spirit appeared at Philippi, when, because Paul
had cast out the spirit of divination which possessed a poor girl
there and thus deprived her masters of a profit, they brought
false charges against Paul and Silas, that they were breaking
the laws of Rome and stirring up sedition, and had them cast
into prison. The magistrates did not take the time to make
much of an investigation, never imagining that at least one of
these strolling mendicant preachers was a Roman citizen, but
had them stripped of their clothes and cruelly beaten. In the
catalogue of his woes and sufferings, Paul afterwards wrote,
"Thrice was I beaten with rods." This cruel outrage at Philippi
was the first of those beatings. It was a barbarous and ferocious
form of punishment under which the victim not infrequently

succumbed, the kind of scourging to which Christ Himself was subjected by Pilate. Faint and bleeding from their wounds, Paul and Silas were cast into prison, into the innermost dungeon, a dark and foul den, where their hands and feet and necks were made fast in the stocks. Their situation was the last word in human misery and distress. How did they take it?

John in a dungeon lost his faith for a little and sent a message of doubt to Jesus. But here is no despair, no rebellion, and no doubt. At midnight Paul and Silas prayed and sang praises unto God, and the prisoners heard them. In their prayers they must have remembered the magistrates who had condemned them, those in Philippi who had come to believe on Jesus, their fellow prisoners, and the jailer himself. I wonder what they were singing? I think one of the songs must have been Psalm 23: "Though I walk through the valley of the shadow of death, I will fear no evil: for thou art with me"; or perhaps Psalm 34: "I will bless the Lord at all times. . . . This poor man cried, and the Lord heard him, and saved him out of all his troubles"; or Psalm 46: "God is our refuge and strength, a very present help in trouble"; or Psalm 102: "For he hath looked down from the height of his sanctuary; from heaven did the Lord behold the earth; to hear the groaning of the prisoner; to loose those that are appointed to death." Paul knew well the promise of the Old Testament, "God . . . giveth songs in the night." Now that promise was made real in his own life. It's a great hour for us when some verse of the Bible ceases to be rhetoric and becomes a blessed experience.

I have visited jails at midnight and there have heard strange music, the sob of remorse breaking from the breast of a first transgressor, the groan of despair, the appeal of the victim of narcotics, the shriek of the hysterical prostitute, and the malediction of the criminal. This was the kind of music which hitherto had echoed within the walls of this old jail. But now they heard a different melody, and all the prisoners heard them singing. You can never tell where your voice will be heard or how far your influence will go, sometimes to the most unlikely places and persons. These prisoners heard them singing and at first answered with jest and ribald laughter. The child-stealer from Ephesus said, "What angels are these who have come to

our palace?" The robber and bandit from the Egnatian Highway said, "They can sing now, but by the morning, they will
have learned our language and pitched their voices to our music." The murderer from Thessalonica said with an oath,
"Would that this right arm of mine were free, and I would
smash their teeth in with my fist and stop their singing." But
still the apostles sang on, and at length a hush of silence and
wonder fell over the dark and dismal dungeon. Tears stole
down cheeks which long had been strangers to them. Thoughts
of innocence and long forgotten happiness came back to these
hardened criminals, and many a heart grew soft with recollec-
tions of yesterday, and from many a breast came a sigh which
was dangerously near a prayer. The song of Paul and Silas had
reached their hearts.

> Down in the human heart, crushed by the tempter;
> Feelings lie buried that grace can restore.

Perhaps when they were through singing, the bandit of the
Egnatian Way asked them to sing it over again. Perhaps it was
the first time, but certainly not the last, that men have made
such a request.

> Sing them over again to me,
> Wonderful words of life.

Suddenly there was an earthquake which shook the foundations of the prison, broke its doors, and loosed the chains from
every prisoner. There was nothing strange about that. Philippi
was in an earthquake zone, and the time and place were con-
spicuous for convulsions of this nature. When the jailer wak-
ened out of his sleep and saw that the prison doors were open
and took for granted that his prisoners had escaped, he drew
his sword and was about to fall on it, following the example of
other suicides in that vicinity, notably Brutus, who had fled
not with their feet, but with their hands. A jail escape in that
ancient day was a more serious thing than with us today, for
then it meant that a jailer's life was forfeited.
But before the jailer could kill himself Paul cried out, "Do

thyself no harm: for we are all here." What a fine description that is of the Gospel, which has for its mission to save men from the self-inflicted wound and bondage of sin. Amazed to discover that his prisoners had not fled, the jailer cried out, "What must I do to be saved?" He was not asking how he could be saved from the earthquake, for its tremors had passed and he was safe. Neither was he asking how he could be saved from the wrath of Caesar for letting the prisoners escape, because the prisoners were all safe. No, it was from something else than the earthquake's shock and the judgment of Caesar that the jailer desired to be saved. In some way the conviction had been brought home to him that he was lost, and he wanted to know how to be saved. How did he come to have the idea of being saved? Perhaps, when impatiently trying to sleep, he had heard Paul and Silas pray for his salvation. Perhaps he had heard the demented maid who cried out, "These men are the servants of the most high God, which show unto us the way of salvation." But however he had come to the knowledge of it, this jailer knew that there was such a thing as salvation, and he wanted it. What shall I do? And still echoing down the ages comes the quick answer of the apostles, "Believe on the Lord Jesus Christ, and thou shalt be saved." This was followed up by Paul and Silas speaking unto him the Word of the Lord, and telling him the way of eternal life; that is, who Christ was, what He had done, and how He saved men. Then the jailer confessed his faith and, like the other converts in the New Testament, was baptized, for with the heart man believeth and with the mouth confession is made unto life.

OTHER GREAT CONVERSIONS

This conversion was sudden and dramatic. It was accompanied by an earthquake. The converted man was full of excitement, emotion, and alarm. Some great men have been converted that way. One was Paul. Another was Luther, who, terrified by a thunderstorm as he was going through the wood to his home at Erfurt, fell on his knees and determined to give his life to God, which at that time meant entering a monastery. John Newton started toward God while the ship on which he was a passenger was being tossed in a storm on the wild Atlantic. Peter Waldo, generally thought to be the first of the Waldensians, was changed from a carefree man of the world to a servant of Christ when a friend who was seated near him at a banquet in Lyons fell dead, and Waldo asked himself, "Where would I now be if it had been I who had fallen dead?" One of the most eloquent of Presbyterian divines of the last century left college and entered the Civil War a skeptic, proud of his unbelief. But when in battle a cannon ball annihilated his companion, who was lying with him face down on the earth during an artillery bombardment, his unbelief and skepticism were blown up, and he entered the ministry. Some come into the Kingdom of God by the earthquake gate.

But others come in other ways. As if to make that clear, we have side by side here in the same chapter the story of the conversion of the first two converts of Europe, one this man who came to God with an earthquake, and the other Lydia, the purple seller, devout and prayerful, whose heart the Lord opened. She came as naturally and noiselessly as the coming of the morning. John Bunyan came by the earthquake route, the Slough-of-Despond path; but in his great common sense he was wise enough to know that not everyone had to travel his way. So he tells us of old Mr. Honest, living in the town of Stupidity, who, although that town was three degrees off the sun, was warmed by its rays and started for the Kingdom of Heaven.

There was no doubt about the genuineness of this conversion. It was so genuine that it embraced his whole house. His wife, his children, and his servants all followed the example of the jailer. "I hear my father pray at prayer meeting, but I never hear him pray at home," said a young man of his father. But the real thing will make a man pray, not only at prayer meeting, but in his own house. This conversion was one which brought forth fruit. What a picture that is, this jailer, in the best room of his own house, in the light of flickering torches, tenderly sponging with his own hands the bleeding backs of Paul and Silas, and then setting before them the best that his house had to offer, and they the very men whom he had thrust into the innermost dungeon and left without bread and water to their misery! A true conversion breaks up the hard places in a man's heart. It makes the cruel man a kind man, and the unjust man a just man.

The great question of the jailer and the great answer of the apostle is a splendid illustration of the way of salvation. Who is responsible for this word "save" and its corresponding word "lost"? Christ Himself. It was He who said, "The Son of man is come to seek and to *save* that which was *lost*"; and it was Christ Himself who was responsible for the answer which Paul gave to the jailer when he told him he could be saved by faith in Christ. There is no other way by which man can be saved. When Jesus, in that great scene of repentance and conversion before He had died on the cross, dismissed the woman who was a sinner, He said, "Thy faith hath saved thee; go in peace."

Just what faith is, and how it saves a man, Paul made clear in his midnight sermon to the alarmed jailer. He did not stop with telling him merely, "Believe, and thou shalt be saved." He explained to him, we may be sure, for he spoke to him the word of the Lord, who Christ is, and what He has done for the sinner. Faith ultimately and finally means faith in Christ's saving work on the cross. To believe in Christ is to believe in Him as the Savior from sin. Until you take Christ in that way and in that great sense, you have never really received Him. You may believe in Him as God's Son, or as a great and even divine Friend, Teacher, and Companion; but you have not really believed on Him until you believe on Him as your Savior.

We Are Saved by Faith

That faith is the only way to be saved is clearly shown when we take the great passages of Scriptures dealing with this subject, and where the word "believe" is used, substitute for it its Greek equivalent "have faith." The verb "believe" always comes from the noun "faith." Take these passages as examples, where we substitute "have faith" for "believe": "God so loved the world, that he gave his only begotten Son, that whosoever *hath faith* in him should not perish, but have everlasting life." "Verily, verily, I say unto you, He that *hath faith* on me hath everlasting life." "Go ye into all the world, and preach the gospel to every creature. He that *hath faith* and is baptized shall be saved." "What must I do to be saved? . . . *Have faith* on the Lord Jesus Christ, and thou shalt be saved." The offer of salvation is free; the gate to heaven is as wide as the mercy of God. But this free salvation is not unconditional. It has one, only one, but nevertheless *one* condition—the sinner's faith in Christ.

Since we are saved by faith, we know that our own character and our own good works have nothing to do with it. If Paul had told this jailer he could be saved by his past record, it would have been a message of despair, for he had no good works to which he could point. In the second place, such a way of salvation by faith in Christ signally honors the Son of God. God chooses not only to save man, but to save him in a way which shall glorify His Son. In the third place, this way of salvation is for us a free way and an easy way. Christ did the hard part. His were the tears, the groans, the sighs, the agony, the cross, and the awful darkness. It is because the way was so hard for Christ that it is so easy for you. Indeed, so easy that some miss it altogether.

What a Christ we have in whom to have faith! To whom shall we go but unto Him? Do you believe? Then prove it, as this jailer did by his acts of mercy and kindness and the joy of his heart. If you have not believed, will you not now believe? Why wait for that and for him who is waiting for you? Do not question the truth of it. Do not be kept back by a lack of feeling or the lack of a good record or a lack of what you think is fit repentance. What Christ said, what Paul said to the jailer, was not to *feel* this way or that way, *do* this or that, lay claim to this or that good act in the past, but *believe*, have faith in the Lord Jesus Christ, and thou shalt be saved. We cannot measure all that "have faith" means. But neither can we measure all that "thou shalt be saved" means. Perhaps, indeed, the jailer by this time could tell you and me something about it. But all that it does mean, for that we shall have to wait until we stand by the jailer's side before the throne of the Lamb and sing our praise unto Him who came to seek and to save that which was lost.

6

WHY?

"If the Lord be with us, why then is all this befallen us?" (Judges 6:13)

Why is one of the great and mysterious words of the Bible and of life. It was the word upon the lips of the righteous Job in the midst of his multiplied sorrows and adversities. Job did not curse God, but he did curse the day he was born and cried out, "Why died I not from the womb?" "Why" was the word that our Savior spoke in His agony upon the cross, "My God, my God, why hast thou forsaken me?" Here the "why" was the word upon the lips of Gideon when the angel called him to deliver the land out of the hand of the Midianites and told him that the Lord was with him. If that was so, Gideon wanted to know *why* all these evils had befallen the land.

Perhaps the most interesting and familiar, and certainly the most important, sight that one sees in the Near East is the threshing floor, for it is a symbol of man's struggle for bread. All over the land during the summer season you can see the oxen or other animals making their monotonous rounds on the threshing floor, and men, children, and women, with their colorful headdress and bright garments, pitching the trampled grain into the air for the wind to carry off the chaff.

But this was a different kind of threshing floor. There was no gaiety; there was no family or community gathering. In a remote glen by a winepress, near the oak in Ophrah, a young man is secretly beating out the grain, not with oxen but with a flail. The reason for this secret operation is the invasion of the Midianites, who have swarmed over the land and have taken possession of the threshing floors wherever they can find one. The face of the young man is dark with sorrow, resentment, and anger as he beats out the grain.

Presently a stranger appears and accosts him, saying, "The Lord is with thee, thou mighty man of valor!" At that, Gideon, for it is none other than he, looks up and says in effect, partly in astonishment and partly in irony, "The Lord be with me, indeed! How can that be? If the Lord is with us, why has He forsaken our land? Come, look out between these two jutting rocks. Yonder is the fertile plain of Esdraelon. There was a day when at this season of the year you might see the dust going up from hundreds of threshing floors, but now not one. The Midianites have come in and swept them clean. Not only have the Midianites taken the threshing floors and the fields, but they have brought in their idols, and even by my father's house there is a grove and an unclean image of Baal. If God is with us, then why has all this happened? I have heard our fathers talk of the great miracles which God wrought in the past for His people, how He brought us up out of Egypt with a mighty hand. But today, when we are oppressed by the Midianites, He doesn't seem to care. Perhaps He is not able to stop it. If the Lord be with us, why then is all this befallen us?"

"Why?" That word spoken by Gideon to the angel on the secret threshing floor in Israel's remote glen thousands of years ago still goes up to heaven. Still it is spoken to all those who come or speak as the messengers of God. From corridors of hospitals, from open graves where the blossoms and the flowers of springtime contrast with death's silence and stillness, from quiet Gethsemanes where troubled souls kneel before their cup, from a thousand battlefields goes up this cry, "Why?" How long, O Lord, how long? Why does God permit it? How can He permit evil men so to curse and darken human life? Why does He permit this devastation of modern Midianites? Why does truth have to fight so hard with error? Why does God seem to be silent unto us, as silent as the stars which look down on the world's woe?

He hides Himself so wondrously
  As though there were no God:
He is least seen when all the powers
  Of ill are most abroad.

Or He deserts us at the hour
  The fight is all but lost,
And seems to leave us to ourselves
  Just when we need Him most.

—F. W. Faber

CONSIDERATIONS THAT HELP

The first consideration that helps when we hear this cry, or when we utter it ourselves—Why has all this happened?—is to remember that here we know in part and we prophesy in part; we see as in a glass darkly. It is not the plan of God that we should be able to answer ourselves all the questions that we ask. I had a devout old elder in a former church who told a person who asked him some difficult, unanswerable questions about the government of God: "If I knew that, I would know as much as God Himself." But we cannot know as much as God. He made known His ways unto Moses, and yet even Moses at the end of his life had to ask "Why?" when God refused to permit him to cross over into the Promised Land. Often his ways are past finding out. Often "His way is in the sea."

There is a very helpful statement that is made in the book of Deuteronomy: "The secret things belong unto the Lord our God: but those things which are revealed belong unto us and to our children forever." There is a "thus far and no farther" to the inquiry of man. We cannot expect to know the things which are hidden with God. This is a part of the human lot. It is certainly part of our human trial. We would have no need of faith if it were not so. Even the Son of God, who drank the cup of man's sorrow and sin, passed into the shadows with a "Why?" upon His lips—"My God, my God, why hast thou forsaken me?"

The second consideration that helps when the anguish of the world asks this question, "Why?" is the fact of sin and judgment. We do not mean that all suffering is the direct result of transgression. The history of Job refutes that, and Christ, in his comment on the fall of the tower of Siloam, dismissed the idea that the victims of that catastrophe were greater sinners than other men.

But the divine law also teaches that sin does bring suffering and judgment and that the sins of a few can bring suffering upon the many. That is certainly true in the world today. In a sense the whole tragedy of human life is due to man's sin and fall and what has come out of it. Men and nations have sinned, and because they have sinned they suffer. We have become too easy in our thought of God. We seem to have the conviction that God is indifferent to sin, that after all He does not care, that men and nations can do as they please and suffer no consequences. But you do not find that in the Bible. That is not the Bible's idea of God. He is a merciful and long-suffering God, but He is also a jealous God and of purer eyes than to behold iniquity. He is a God who does terrible things in righteousness.

That was recognized at a great crisis in the history of our own nation when there was deep suffering throughout the land. Speaking with the inspiration of an old Testament prophet, Abraham Lincoln in his second inaugural address said:

> The Almighty has his own purposes. Woe unto the world because of offenses, for it must needs be that offenses come; but woe to that man by whom the offense comes. Fondly do we hope, fervently do we pray that this mighty scourge of war may speedily pass away. Yet if God wills that it continue until all the wealth piled by the bondsman's two hundred and fifty years of unrequitted toil shall be sunk, and until every drop of blood drawn with the lash shall be paid by another drawn with the sword, as was said three thousand years ago, so still it must be said, "The judgments of the Lord are true and righteous altogether."

The third consideration which will help us is to remember that this is not the first time the question "Why has this happened?" has been asked. It has been asked from age to age, wherever sin has darkened human life, wherever men have drunk their cup of woe. Whether suggested by personal vicissitudes or by the burden of sorrow that rests upon mankind, there is nothing new about this question, "Why?" The prophets asked it. Gideon asked it. Elijah asked it. David asked it. Christ Himself asked it. There is nothing peculiar in our situation. Whatever personal troubles there have been, whatever waves of war and desolation have swept over the earth, men have always asked "Why?" And yet grandly from age to age have gone up the psalms and hymns of man's faith in God.

> Who roll'd the psalm to wintry skies,
> Who built him fanes of fruitless prayer,
>
> Who trusted God was love indeed
> And love Creation's final law,
> Tho' Nature, red in tooth and claw
> With ravine, shrieked against his creed.
>
> —Tennyson, *In Memoriam*

The believers of all past ages had as much and more to trouble their faith as we do today; yet they endured as seeing Him who is invisible. Shall not we also endure?

If, like the psalmist, you are troubled when you think upon God and relate His being and His government to what goes on in the world, how much more will you be troubled by the alternative? And what is the alternative? The alternative is a world without God, a world with suffering and catastrophe, and yet a world without God and without hope. A troubled faith is better than no faith at all. Think of what it would be like if we had to look out upon our troubled, suffering world without any faith in God, without any hope that God guides the movements of the world.

> Yet there is less to try our faith
> In our mysterious creed,
> Than in the godless look of earth
> In these our hours of need.
>
> —F. W. Faber

The final consideration is that out of evil God will bring good. God is not so silent as we think He is. We have God's Word, God's speech, in the Bible, and this is a truth that He utters over and over again in the Bible, that He can overrule evil for good, that He can use even the most wicked men and the most wicked transactions for His purposes, that He is able to make the wrath of man to praise Him and the residue He will restrain. God never resigns His throne. The sun and stars never fall out of heaven, although we may not be able to see them on certain days because of the clouds which obscure them. But the sun and the moon and the stars are still there. And so back of all the clouds and shadows the earth has seen is the holy, everliving, and omnipotent God. No good, spiritual, moral thing has ever been destroyed or ever can be destroyed. The things which can be shaken down, and ought to be shaken down, are from time to time shaken down, that the things which cannot be shaken shall remain. Out of the trouble, turmoil, strife, anguish, sorrow, and sin of the ages is to come at length the New Jerusalem, the holy city of God, wherein dwelleth righteousness.

OUR PART

Instead of asking "Why?" our part is to repent and to humble ourselves under the mighty hand of God. When some thought that the men on whom the tower of Siloam fell, or the men whose blood Pilate mingled with the blood of the burnt offerings in the temple, were greater sinners than other men, Christ said, "Except ye repent, ye shall all likewise perish." The world is slow to repent, unwilling to be torn from its idols, and likewise the heart of man. Let us search our hearts and repent of our sins and be sure that we shall not be found to be fighting against God.

The storm is the time when the ship is tested, not the calm. The world storm is a time for the testing of our faith in God and in His Kingdom. When the storm was raging at its wildest and everyone on the ship had given up hope, Paul stood forth and said, "Sirs, be of good cheer. I believe God." This is a time for those who believe in God to show it.

Instead of asking "Why is there so much trouble and sorrow and pain in the world?" our duty as individuals is to do what we can to mitigate and alleviate that sorrow and suffering. What answer did this angel give to Gideon when he asked his troubled question, "O my lord, if the Lord be with us, why then is all this befallen us, and where be all his miracles which our fathers told us of, saying, Did not the Lord bring us up from Egypt? But now the Lord hath forsaken us, and delivered us into the hands of the Midianites"? What was the answer the angel gave? Did he enter into a theological discussion and attempt to justify the ways of God with man? No, not that! He gave him no answer, but he gave him a command. He told him to act, to act against the invader whose blight was on the land, to act against the idolatry that defiled even his father's house. "Go in this thy might, and thou shalt save Israel from the hand of the Midianites: have not I sent thee?" The question is not what answer you can give to the mystery of the world's woe and suffering, but, what are you doing about it? What resistance are you making to evil in your own life and in the life of the world? What part do you take in the binding up of the wounds of mankind?

I remember a great many things that my mother told me, but nothing more than this: When she was troubled by the thought of the world's sorrow and pain and by the thought of so many persons dying without the knowledge of the truth and entering into a Christless eternity, the word that came to her was always this, as if Christ were speaking to her soul: "I gave my life for the world. What are you doing for it?"

7

WHAT WILT THOU HAVE ME TO DO?

"And [Saul], trembling and astonished, said, Lord, what wilt thou have me to do?" (Acts 9:6)

It is always interesting to look at turning points and study the forces which have determined the course of a great life. Here it was a question which changed the man's life and turned it into new channels. When we consider who it was that asked the question, and the results and the issue of the question, we can say that this was the greatest question ever asked.

Never was there a man who up to that moment felt less need of asking such a question. Never was there a man whose path was plainer before him. Never a man more sure of his purpose and his goal in life or more determined to reach it. And yet this man was the man who asked the question: "Lord, what wilt thou have me to do?"

From his youth up he had been devoted to the study and the maintenance of the religion of Israel. Born a Hebrew of the Hebrews, and of the straitest sect of the Pharisees, his gifts and his character early marked him for distinction. He was sent up to study the sacred law at Jerusalem, where he sat at the feet of Gamaliel. In the Christian Gospel he saw only a blasphemous assault on the faith of the fathers, and in Jesus a wicked impostor. Everywhere he spoke and acted against the

Christian disciples, and at the stoning of Stephen he held the garments of those who stoned that first martyr. Against all the followers of Jesus he was, he tells us, afterwards, "exceedingly mad," "breathing out threatenings and slaughter" against them. Because of his zeal and energy he soon became the chief of the persecutors and the chief of the enemies of the church. He was not content with his conquest at Jerusalem, but having heard that the odious heresy had broken out at Damascus, he started thither, armed with authority to arrest and drag into prison those who confessed the name of Jesus. His was a fury that spared neither age nor sex.

But now came the great question and the great change. As he drew near to the hoary city of Damascus, with snow-crowned Hermon looming up in the distance, suddenly a bright light shone from heaven, a light so bright that it blinded him, and the fierce persecutor fell helpless to the ground. As he lay there he heard a voice which said, "Saul, Saul, why persecutest thou me?" The astonished Saul replied, "Who art thou, Lord?" Then the voice said, "I am Jesus whom thou persecutest." To this Saul answered, "Lord, what wilt thou have me to do?" Then he was told what he was to do. He had been chosen to know the just One, to be a chosen vessel unto Christ and witness to His name before the Gentiles and the kings and the children of Israel, to open their eyes and turn them from darkness to light, and from the power of Satan unto God that they might receive forgiveness of sins. He was also told that he was to suffer great things for the sake of the name of Jesus.

All this was the direct opposite of what he had been doing. Never was a man turned more completely about. He was told to preach as the Son of God and Messiah the very Jesus whom he had reviled; to build up the church he had tried to destroy; to spread the Gospel that he detested; to plead with men to come to Christ, instead of imprisoning and slaying them for believing on Him. That was what Saul was now commanded to do. But by the grace of God he did it. He was "not disobedient unto the heavenly vision." Saul became Paul and began to write the greatest chapter in the history of mankind.

"What wilt thou have me to do?" This is an appropriate question for every Christian to ask. In our best moments all of us, I think, would like to do the will of God. That is man's highest achievement. Even Jesus said that it was His "meat . . . to do the will of him that sent me." Where the will of God is done, there we have the Kingdom of God.

THE WORK OF LIFE

This is a question that is in the minds of young men and young women as they face life. "What wilt thou have me to do?" Here is the field of life and of time. The field is wide, but time is short, and I have only one life to live. How can I best invest my talent? How can I best invest my desire to serve God and do good to my fellow man? There is no joy superior to that of doing what one likes to do and which also does good to man and serves God.

In asking this question about the work of life, we ought not to pass by what may be spoken of as the primary and fundamental callings of life, and without which there would be no other occupation. By this I mean the work of the laborer, the miner, the merchant and storekeeper who distribute the necessities of life; and above all, or underneath all, the work of the farmer. How true it is what the wise man said of old, "The king himself is served by the field." These fundamental callings of life can be followed, and at the same time the higher interests of life and the mind cultivated. At a gathering at Pomona College on the Pacific coast, where the theme for the discussion was the so-called "humanities," one of the speakers said that all education ought to deal with practical things. He wanted his son to know how to do practical things, how for example to milk a cow. He was followed by another speaker who said that he too wanted his boy to know how to do practical things, and how to milk a cow, but he would also like him to know how to do some things that a calf can't do better.

Then there are the so-called learned professions: law, medicine, science, teaching, the ministry. All these offer high opportunities to serve one's day and generation. Great is the influence of a Christian teacher or professor, a Christian lawyer, a Christian doctor. At a banquet held in honor of certain celebrities in the athletic world, one of those who received great acclaim was Tyrus Cobb, the famous baseball star of twenty-five years ago. A minister said to Cobb as they were leaving the banquet hall, "It must be a source of great joy and pride to you to receive such praise as you have heard tonight, and to know that you have given entertainment as a ballplayer to so many thousands of people." At that a wistful look came over the face of the famous ballplayer as he said, "I wish that I had been a doctor. To have been able to heal diseases and relieve people of pain would have meant far more to me than the cheers and plaudits of the thousands in baseball parks."

When it comes to the professions, I would like to say a word for the ministry. As a class, ministers are the most poorly compensated of all professional men. And yet they have compensations of a higher order. It is the minister's opportunity to guide and inspire youth. An engineer who received sometime ago the highest decoration that an American engineer can receive, in accepting the medal, said, "It was an old preacher down in Texas who lighted the fire in me." That sometimes the preacher will do. He will light the fire of ambition and high desire in the mind of some youth. It is his privilege also to counsel in the time of perplexity and temptation, to say a word which will keep someone from taking the wrong turning and starting on a path which will bring misery and sorrow. As a reverend champion it is his office to cheer the sick, to encourage the discouraged, to comfort the sorrowing, and to soften, as far as it can be softened, the blow of death, and kindle a light of faith and hope in life's western sky. And what joy could be comparable to that of being used of God unto the salvation of an immortal soul?

The minister is not only one who has the opportunity to do good to his fellow men, but he stands in their presence as an appointed messenger of God, one who is to speak not his own words, but the Word of God. What could be equal to that, to stand, even the lowest and humblest, in that long succession of men who have proclaimed the Word of the Lord, whether he does it from a metropolitan pulpit in the midst of the great city or from the pulpit of a little frame church in the country at the crossroads, under the shadow of the swaying branches of the oak and the hickory trees? This is why the true pulpit, where the Word of God is spoken,

> Must stand acknowledg'd, while the world shall stand,
> The most important and effectual guard,
> Support, and ornament of Virtue's cause.
> There stands the messenger of truth: there stands
> The legate of the skies—His theme divine,
> His office sacred, his credentials clear.
> By him the violated law speaks out
> Its thunders; and by him, in strains as sweet
> As angels use, the Gospel whispers peace!
> —William Cowper, *The Task*

But whatever work in life is chosen, and whatever calling a man follows, in that calling he can honor God and do good to his fellow man. For every one of us there is a particular work to do. On the front of the house on the hilltop in Pittsburgh, where Pittsburgh's famous astronomer and instrument maker John Brashear made his first telescopes, is this inscription, not original with Brashear, but one which he liked to quote for the benefit of young men: "Somewhere beneath the stars is a work which you alone were meant to do. Never rest until you have found it."

THE IMPORTANT CHOICES AND DECISIONS OF LIFE

"Lord, what wilt thou have me to do?" This is a question which will often be asked by an earnest soul when facing some important choice or decision. No moral issue is involved; and yet the one about to make the decision realizes that it will have a profound influence upon his life. Take the matter of marriage. With regard to this step in life the question "What wilt thou have me to do?" is ever timely, and especially so today, when about one out of every three marriages goes on the rocks. One of the reasons why they turn out that way is because the couples have not asked, "Lord, what wilt thou have me to do?" Too many couples today go from the cocktail party to the marriage altar, instead of from their knees. "Wilt thou go with this man?"

This question, as we saw in an earlier sermon, is one of the most important questions of life. Will this man, will this woman, strengthen me or weaken me in my Christian life? That is something that ought not to be forgotten. But where the way is clear and the conviction strong, then none ought to be afraid to answer that question the way Rebekah answered it of old, "I will go!" Once I talked with a retired medical missionary. He had served for many years in the African Congo. His wife was a cultivated and still youthful-looking woman, and one could easily imagine how attractive she must have been when he asked her, "Wilt thou go?" She answered, "I will go," and followed him across the seas to the African Congo, to minister to the lowest of the low amid the African bush.

Then there is the matter of some particular decision: the taking or the refusal of a certain post; the choice of a residence. Or it may be some difficult domestic matter where a decision must be made and a course followed; or some personal relationship. Who has not come face-to-face with these matters and said earnestly, "Lord, what wilt thou have me to do?"

I have heard people tell of how it was their custom to open the Bible at random, and of the comfort and guidance they found in some appropriate verse. When the great Russian writer Dostoevski was on his deathbed and wanted to know whether this was the end or not, he asked his wife to bring him the old worn Bible, the only book which he was permitted to have when he was in exile in Siberia. Opening it at random, his eye fell upon the words of Matthew 3:15, the words of Jesus to John when he baptized Him: "Suffer it to be so now." Dostoevski took that to mean that the end of his life had come. I would not discourage anyone from such a use of the Bible. And yet, opening the Bible at random, you might chance upon a verse which had no meaning at all for your situation or which would seem to have the wrong meaning, as when John Wesley, in doubt as to whether or not he should join Whitefield in preaching to the colliers of Bristol, opened the Bible at random and read this verse: "And devout men carried Stephen to his burial." Then a Moravian friend tried it for him with no greater success, for the verse to which he opened was this: "And Ahaz slept with his fathers." On the other hand, on the day of his great change, May 24, 1738, Wesley opened his Bible at chance and read the timely and encouraging words: "Thou art not far from the kingdom of God." The best way to use the Bible, however, is to read it for the guidance which comes out of the great truths and principles which it proclaims. In matters where no moral issue is involved, and yet where you cannot be certain which way to turn, the best that you can do is to choose one course and leave the rest to God, trusting in His providence.

THE DENIALS AND FRUSTRATIONS OF LIFE

When confronted by some denial or frustration in life, the soul will sometimes ask the question, "Lord, what wilt thou have me to do? You have closed this door against me. Why is it so? What is it that thou wilt have me to do?"

That was a question that Paul must have asked not infrequently, for there were many frustrations and denials in his life. He had that thorn in the flesh, perhaps a disease of the eyes, or some other painful and humiliating and hindering affliction. Three times he earnestly besought God to take this thorn from him. No doubt he wondered why God permitted such an affliction when he was so anxious to preach the Gospel. The prayer was not granted, the thorn was not plucked. But Paul learned that this thorn was God's final will for him, and it became to him a source of strength. When he was weak he said, "Then am I strong." For that reason he could take pleasure in his infirmity and glory in it, that the power of Christ might rest upon him.

John Milton, in the day of his denial and frustration, asked that same question, "Lord, why is this burden laid upon me? What wilt thou have me to do?"

> "Doth God exact day-labor, light denied?"
> I fondly ask. But Patience, to prevent
> That murmur, soon replies: "God doth not need
> Either man's work or his own gifts; who best
> Bear his mild yoke, they serve him best; his state

Is kingly: thousands at his bidding speed,
And post o'er land and ocean without rest;
They also serve who only stand and wait."
                    —John Milton, *Sonnet on His Blindess*

The supreme illustration of doing God's will by submitting to it in trust and love is that of Jesus Himself. He not only taught us to pray, "Thy will be done," but in the Garden of Gethsemane, in His sore agony when He knelt before His cup and prayed, "If it be possible, let this cup pass from me," He concluded His prayer by saying, "Nevertheless not as I will, but as thou wilt." So for you too it is possible to serve and glorify God by submitting to His will. Thus for all eternity, by uniting your will with that of God, you become a coworker with God.

IN THE MIDST OF A WRONG COURSE IN LIFE

Paul was on the wrong path and doing the wrong thing, although at that time he was not conscious of it when he heard the voice of Jesus, "Why persecutest thou me?" and asked his great question, "What wilt thou have me to do?" The moment he knew he was wrong, Paul turned about, asked God which way to go, and when the way was made plain, took it immediately. When you find yourself on a wrong path and God has made plain His way and His will to you, then there is only one thing to do, and that is to take that way and to take it at once. Paul said that when he heard the voice of God, when he asked the question, "What wilt thou have me to do?" and got the answer, he was "not disobedient unto the heavenly vision." But alas, how many there are to whom, in one way or another, not perhaps by a blinding light like that which flashed and flamed on the Damascan highway, but in ways just as clear, God speaks His warning and shows His way, yet who are not obedient to that heaven-sent vision, but go on in the wrong path, a path which can lead only to sorrow and shame and misery.

There is one thing that stands out in all this record of Paul's conversion, and that is that God wanted him to come to Christ. That was God's will for Paul. It is God's will for you and me too. For God is not willing that any should perish, but that all should come to repentance. That is the will of God for you. Have you done that? Have you repented? Have you come to Christ? Take this as your motto: "Lord, what wilt thou have me to do?" There is only one thing in the future to fear—that is not to do the will of God.

8

IS THE YOUNG MAN SAFE?

"The king said unto Cushi, Is the young man Absalom safe?" (2 Samuel 18:32)

It was sunrise in the wild mountain country across the Jordan. In front of the fortress of Mahanaim, the king of Israel, David, driven out of his capital by the rebellion of Absalom, stood to review his troops as they marched toward the field of battle. There were three divisions of veteran soldiers: one under Abishai, another under Ittai, and the third under the captain of the host, Joab himself. The earth shook beneath the tread of these thousands of armed men. Trumpets sounded, flags and pennants streamed in the morning wind, helmet and shield and spear flashed in the bright sunlight. As each division came abreast of David, it halted to salute the king. Before it passed on David said a word to each commander. That word was this: "Deal gently for my sake with the young man, even with Absalom." Then the trumpets spoke once more, and the army marched on toward the battle, leaving behind it a cloud of dust. Soon the army with its three divisions vanished into the wood of Ephraim.

All day long David paced up and down before the fortress, refusing meat and drink and conversation with his officers and guard, for his heart was in the great battle raging in the wood of Ephraim. At length the watchman on top of the tower above David reported a runner approaching in the distance. The runner was Ahimaaz, who had started after Joab had sent the first and official runner Cushi with dispatches for the king and tidings of the battle. When the runner drew near to David he called out, "Blessed be the Lord thy God, which hath delivered up the men that lifted up their hand against my lord the king." But that was not what the king was thinking about; that was not what he wanted to know. What he was thinking about, and what was on his heart, was the fate of Absalom. So he said to Ahimaaz, "Is the young man Absalom safe?" Ahimaaz knew only that a great victory had been won over the rebel army; but he knew nothing of the fate of Absalom and answered the king, "I saw a great tumult, but I knew not what it was." David said to him, "Turn aside, and stand here."

After a little the second runner, the Cushite, appeared in the distance. When he came panting up to where the king stood, he cried out, "Tidings, my lord the king: for the Lord hath avenged thee this day of all them that rose up against thee." Then came the question that was on David's heart: "Is the young man Absalom safe?" The Cushite runner knew what had happened to Absalom and told David the truth: "The enemies of my lord the king, and all that rise up against thee to do thee hurt, be as that young man is." When David heard that, he wrapped his mantle about him and, climbing the stone stairway to the chamber over the gate, wept and lamented as he went, "O my son Absalom, my son, my son Absalom! Would God I had died for thee, O Absalom, my son, my son!"

No, it was not well with Absalom. The young man was not safe. When he was fleeing from the field of battle on his royal mule, his luxuriant hair, admired by all, the pride of Absalom and which he polled every year and which weighed two hundred shekels, caught in the low-hanging branches of an oak tree, and the mule ran on, leaving Absalom suspended by his hair. When they came upon him, Joab took three darts and drove it through the rebel's heart. With his sword he slashed through the golden locks of hair, letting the body fall to the ground. Then it was cast into a deep pit. As the victorious soldiers of David marched past the pit on their way from the field of battle, each man took a stone and, with an execration, hurled it down upon the body of Absalom until a great heap of stones marked the place where his body lay. But that was not the tomb that Absalom had prepared for himself. He had reared for himself a costly mauso-leum, known as Absalom's Pillar, in the king's dale. That was the tomb which he expected to occupy. There his flawless body, arrayed in magnificent royal robes and anointed for the sepul-cher, was to be laid away with a kingdom's lamentation. Suc-ceeding generations were to tarry by that tomb and exclaim, "Here lies Absalom, the son of David!" But how different was the grave into which Absalom was cast like a dead dog! There at the bottom of the pit, covered with the heap of stones and with none save his brokenhearted father to mourn over him, lay that once-flawless body without a blemish from the sole of his foot to the crown of his head, all gashed and broken and mutilated. But yonder in the king's dale stands his pillar and mausoleum. The rising sun gilds with glory its finely chiseled stone, its silver and its gold. The noonday sun halts to behold its beauty, and night drapes its white shaft with her ethereal robe. But it is a tomb without an occupant, a pillar without a prince, a monu-ment without a man.

Absalom was not safe. He had high position, personal beauty, charm, and eloquence, so that he was able to steal the hearts of the people. He had lofty ambition, not only for this world but after his death; and yet there lies his body, broken and mangled, covered with stones of shame and derision at the bottom of the forest pit.

"Is the young man safe?" This is a question which is asked by many fathers and mothers, and by sons too. Conscience, faithful conscience, will often whisper to the heart of the young man, striving to win him back from an evil way, "Is the young man safe?" Life is a dangerous territory. It has been so from the very beginning. There was a dangerous tree in the midst of the Gar-den of Eden. Because of these dangers many come to a disastrous end, with some father, mother, sister, wife lamenting over them.

THE PERILS OF THE BUSINESS WORLD

This is the world that the great majority of young men must enter. It is the world that keeps the world moving; yet it has its dangers. There is the danger of esteeming financial and busi-ness success as the great end of life and forgetting the higher success, the success of the soul. Over the old fireplaces in old homes one would often see a rifle or a sword. These were symbols of struggle and sacrifice and conquest. But no one ever saw a yardstick suspended over a fireplace. If you go through a cemetery, you will see all kinds of emblems and read all kinds of inscriptions. But there is one thing that you have never seen inscribed on any tombstone, and that is a dollar sign. When it comes to the finalities of life, life must be thought of in other terms than the terms of money.

There is the danger too in the business world of compromising with the standards of the age and of the world. Court statistics show an appalling increase in the number of forgeries and stealings. Therefore it is that the young man from the very beginning, to be safe, must resolve to be loyal to conscience.

THE PERILS OF THE SOCIAL WORLD

One of these is gambling. A biography of the great Russian novelist Dostoevski reveals the havoc and misery that came into his life through gambling. Time and time again it brought him into terrible straits, and on one occasion he went even so far as to steal the jewels of his wife and pawn them that he might take a chance in the casino. Gambling today may be described as the national American vice. Men bet on everything from ball games to numbers on the stock markets. It is so easy for a young man to get started on that course. No one is safe who takes that path. Nothing will so eat out the character and fiber of a man as the passion of gambling.

Another social peril for the young man—and for the young woman—today is the peril of drinking. No one starts to drink simply because he wants to drink or has any taste or desire for liquor. On the contrary, the body of man at the beginning has a strong aversion to intoxicating drink. The way men start to drink is because they are invited to do so by others. They want to be good fellows, go along with the crowd and be popular. I talked once with a man who was in a dangerous condition, a condition brought on through drink; and he was about to lose all that was of worth in life. After he had signed a pledge, I asked him how he got started on such a course. He said that he had been a bank clerk, naming one of the principal banks in the city. He had never taken a drink of liquor, but at the annual banquet of the bank at one of the hotels liquor was served. He went along with the crowd and drank. That was the beginning of his downfall. He did not want to be thought odd or strange, and so he committed the unspeakable folly of letting others override his principles. Alas, how often that tragedy takes place! No one is more interested in the welfare of your soul than yourself. Why, then, follow others in a dangerous course and go against your own soul? What do those others care about your welfare? An intoxicated woman was picked up recently on the steps of a church. She was given kind treatment and assistance and sent in a cab to her hotel. The explanation she gave of her predicament was that she wanted to be popular, and thus she started on that evil path.

Once men were everywhere warned against the peril of drinking. Boys and girls had that warning in school in the course and teaching in physiology which displayed the effects of liquor upon a man's body. Sermons were preached on the subject. There were temperance bands and societies; books, and even plays, like *Ten Nights in a Bar Room*, warned the young man against liquor. But how different it is today! Suppose a messenger from Mars were to come and visit our world, what would be his conclusion? When he drove along our highways and saw the great illuminated liquor signs? When he listened on a radio and heard the programs introduced by a liquor advertisement? When he picked up the widely circulated magazines and saw page after page of costly and artistic advertisements of different brands of whisky and beer? When he went to a public banquet and found that the chief speakers and distingnished guests all gathered to drink cocktails before the banquet started? When he went to get a meal and found that there was hardly a place where liquor was not sold and displayed? What would be the conclusion of this messenger from Mars? His conclusion would be, after seeing and listening to all this display and praise of strong drink, that drinking is the great end to be desired and is the fountain of life's chief blessing. But how contrary is the fact. Still, as of old, drink is the great enemy of man's body, of his mind, of his soul, of his welfare and peace. Still there is no need to revise that ancient verdict: "Wine is a mocker, strong drink is raging: and whosoever is deceived thereby is not wise."

Another social peril is the peril of sex, the throwing together of men and women in every field of life, and now in the field of business. Every passion of man has a tempter waiting for it. It was written ages ago, but it is still up-to-date and still warns the young man. Perhaps Solomon, from the roof garden of his palace, saw the very young man whom he describes actually passing through the street on his way to destruction. This is what he saw and what he said: "For at the window of my house I looked through my casement, and beheld among the simple ones, I discerned among the youths, a young man void of understanding, passing through the street near her corner, and he went the way to her house, in the twilight, in the evening, in the black and dark night; and, behold, there met him a woman with the attire of an harlot, and subtil of heart. . . .With her much fair speech she caused him to yield, with the flattering of her lips she forced him. He goeth after her straightway, as an ox goeth to the slaughter, or as a fool to the correction of the stocks; till a dart strike through his liver; as a bird hasteth to the snare, and knoweth not that it is for his life."

Books that formerly could be circulated only clandestinely, and were outlawed in decent society, are now among the best sellers. Unless human nature has changed completely, unless you must answer in the affirmative what human nature and the history of human nature declares must be answered in the negative, that old question, "Can a man take fire into his bosom and not be burned?" then the young man and the young woman who read such kind of books or go to such kind of plays are not safe.

At a church anniversary in New York a good many years ago, one of the chief speakers, a minister, related how one night, thirty years before, he and a companion set out to attend a theater where a vile play was being presented. When they got to the lighted doorway of the theater, both of them had an arresting hand laid upon them by their conscience, their early training, and their past habit, and both turned to go away from the theater. One of the young men, however, after walking along for a little distance, turned about and went back to the theater, bought his ticket, and went in. The other kept his resolution and went back to his boardinghouse. That was the turning point for him. He followed the path of industry and of study and honor and virtue, and for thirty years had led a useful and honorable life as a minister of the Gospel. It was the turning point too for that other young man. He went in and looked and listened and had his passions stirred, and went back again and again until his nature was corrupted and he sank steadily from one misery into another. That same king who saw the young man void of understanding going to his doom wrote these words: "Stolen waters are sweet, and bread eaten in secret is pleasant. But he knoweth not that the dead are there; and that her guests are in the depths of hell."

THE PERILS OF THE MIND

It is natural, because of the state of man's nature, for his mind to revolt against authority and religion. That was so at the very beginning. The tempter came to the man and the woman and said, "Hath God said?" The young man is always subject to the temptation of being caught and attracted by some clever half-truth, some plausible argument, or some brilliant saying of a freethinker or an infidel. Particularly is that true in the atmosphere of the university world today. But in these negations and sneers there is nothing which lays a foundation for life or ennobles and purifies the heart. A laugh or a jest at religion and faith is, as Robert Burns found out, a poor compensation for "Deity offended." The freedom which unbelief promises turns out to be bondage and slavery. How true is that word of Peter, "While they promise them liberty, they themselves are the servants of corruption: for of whom a man is overcome, of the same is he brought in bondage."

We have spoken of the perils in life for the young man. Now, in closing, a word about some of the safeguards for the young man. One is industry and hard work. He can say to the tempter what Nehemiah, the bravest man of the Bible, said to his enemies, who, in order to stop him from building the wall at Jerusalem, tried to entice him into a conference so they could slay him, "I am doing a great work, so that I cannot come down." Another safeguard is high ambition. It must not be ambition for self alone. Absalom had plenty of ambition, but he had no reverence for the higher things, no reverence for God, and no desire to serve his fellow man. But to have such a worthy desire is a great safeguard for the young man.

Right companions are a powerful defense for the young man. Nothing so affects his life for good or evil as the kind of companions he has. When he was in the military school as a young cadet, Napoleon had a companion who was taking the wrong path. He said to him, "I have succeeded in keeping your morals pure. Your new friends will destroy you. Choose between them and me. There is no middle course. Be a man and decide." After a third warning he said to this friend, "You have despised my warnings and renounced my friendship. Never speak to me again." John Wesley had the right idea when he resolved he would have no intimate friends who would not help him on the road to heaven. Call the roll of the young men who have gone down, who have ended in the pit like Absalom, and you will see how the great majority of them got the wrong start with the wrong kind of friend.

The right kind of companionship in marriage is a blessed safeguard for the young man. A young man came once to seek my counsel. He had returned from the army and had fallen in love with a young woman. They became strongly attached to one another and were contemplating marriage. But there was one difficulty. He had an association with one of the secret societies which the young woman regarded as unworthy. She would not marry him unless he broke his connection with this society. To him and to his family the assciation was altogether honorable, and he was not disposed to break his connection with this society.

I said to him, "Do you love this young woman and does she love you? Is she a woman of high character, Christian faith, and conviction?" He said that she was. Then I said, "Do not hesitate. The help and companionship of such a woman will be worth far more to you than your association with this or any other society or secular body."

Chesterton wrote a poem which he called "Music." It is about a young man who was never stirred to greatness and goodness until he had given his heart and hand to a worthy woman. The thought of her summoned him to honor and truth and purity:

> Naught is lost, but all transmuted.
> Years are sealed, but eyes have seen;
> Saw her smile—O soul, be worthy!
> Saw her tears—O heart, be clean!
>
> —G. K. Chesterton

Another mighty safeguard is loyalty to conscience under all circumstances. There is a legend of a knight, Sir Basil, who once went hunting with a company of fellow knights and nobles. He had a falcon on his wrist, as the fashion was. At length he grew weary of the hunt and being thirsty, went to a cliff where a tiny stream was trickling down the side of the rock. He unloosed the falcon from his wrist and it flew up and perched at the top of the cliff. The knight took his hunter's horn, stopped one end of it with moss, and using the horn as an improvised cup, held it so that the tiny stream would drop into it. Just as he was putting the horn to his lips, the falcon dashed down like an arrow and struck the horn out of his hand. The knight picked the horn up and again held it under the drops of water until it was filled. A second time he put the horn to his lips, and again the falcon dashed down and struck the horn out of his hand. The angry knight resolved that if his falcon did it again, he would kill it. He filled his horn the third time, and when the third time the falcon dashed down to strike the vessel out of his hand, the knight struck the bird and killed it. Then he lifted the cup and threw back his head to drink. But as he did so, he saw at the very edge of the cliff, coiled around the rock from under which the water was dripping, a monstrous serpent, the venom and filth of its mouth mingling with the water that had dropped into the horn. Then the knight was grateful to the falcon and sorry that he had killed it. Never strike your conscience! Conscience is your best and most faithful friend.

> What conscience tells me should be done,
>   Or warns me not to do;
> This teach me more than hell to shun,
>   That more than heaven pursue.

And finally there is the great safeguard of religion—the worship of the church, the work of the church, the reading of the Bible, and daily prayer. These are ancient, but tried and mighty, safeguards for the soul. And the reason is that they bring you into the fellowship of the great Companion, the great Friend, the great Savior who said, "He that followeth me shall not walk in darkness."

9

HAVE THE GATES OF DEATH BEEN OPENED UNTO THEE?

"Have the gates of death been opened unto thee?" (Job 38:17)

"I . . . have the keys of hell and of death." (Revelation 1:18)

To that question which the Almighty addressed to him, "Have the gates of death been opened unto thee?" Job could make no answer, save the answer of silence. Outside of Jesus Christ, that is the universal answer. Christ is the only one to whom the gates of death have been opened, and the only one who can open them. Here is His great answer to that great question: "I am he that liveth, and was dead; and, behold, I am alive for evermore, Amen; and have the keys of hell and of death."

Exiled for the testimony of Jesus Christ to the lonely Isle of Patmos, probably in the reign of the Emperor Domitian, John was in the spirit on the Lord's Day and heard behind him a great voice like a trumpet. When he turned to see who was speaking, he saw one standing in the midst of seven golden candlesticks, like unto the Son of Man, His hair and His head white like wool, as white as snow, and His eyes like a flame of fire, and His voice as the sound of many waters. In His right hand He held seven stars, and out of His mouth went a sharp two-edged sword, and His countenance was like the glory of the sun. When John saw this majestic person, although once he had leaned on His breast at the Last Supper, he fell at His feet as one dead. Then the One who had spoken laid His right hand upon him and said, "Fear not; I am the first and the last: I am he that liveth, and was dead; and, behold, I am alive for evermore, Amen; and have the keys of hell and of death."

This is, in some respects, the greatest text in the Bible. All the trumpets of Christian faith are sounding in it, for here we have the eternal and changeless Christ, His atonement for sin, His resurrection from the dead, and His all-conquering Kingdom. It was a great text for John's troubled day, when the Roman empire was seeking to drown the church in its blood. But it is a great text for any age, and certainly for our age and this hour, when the fountains of the great deeps have been broken up and all things are being shaken.

"I AM THE FIRST AND THE LAST"

Elsewhere in this book this same voice, and it is Christ who is speaking, says, "I am Alpha and Omega, the beginning and the end." Christ is before all history as He is after all history. As the Apostle Paul put it, "He is before all things, and by him all things consist." Christ brackets the ages. The history of the world is just a parenthesis between Christ as the beginning and Christ as the end. In the midst of the changes and fluctuations of time the heart of man longs for the changeless, for the unshaken and the unshakable. It is not strange, therefore, that in that early age when the empire was seeking to destroy the church, and when those who confessed Christ were being burned at the stake or exiled like John to the mines or torn to pieces by wild beasts in the arenas or sewed up in sacks with serpents and flung into the sea, believers in Christ should have chosen as one of the favorite symbols of their faith alpha and omega. They believed in and followed a Savior and King who is the "same yesterday, today, and forever."

"I AM HE THAT LIVETH AND WAS DEAD"

That is the first of two great wonders, that the Everliving One should have died. The second of these two great wonders is that the One who died should now be alive forevermore.

He who is the first and the last, Alpha and Omega, He that liveth, died. There you have the atonement of Christ on the cross for our sins. That He who ever liveth also died, is the great paradox in which the writers of the New Testament delighted. "Who, being in the form of God, thought it not robbery to be equal with God: but made himself of no reputation, and took upon him the form of a servant, and was made in the likeness of men: and being found in fashion as a man, he humbled himself, and became obedient unto death, even the death of the cross."

There can be no intelligent or truly helpful commemoration of Easter which does not relate it to this great truth and fact, that He who was living died, and that He died for our sins. As the apostle stated it, He "was delivered for our offences, and was raised again for our justification." We must not look upon Easter with a too exclusive reference to immortality, to life to come, although that is in it. The chief thing is that Easter is the great proof and seal that Christ died for our sins, and that He has overcome the power of sin in human life. We must look upon the resurrection of Jesus as the last act in the great series of acts by which God bestows upon us salvation and eternal life. In Christ crucified we behold Him "who was made a little lower than the angels for the suffering of death, crowned with glory and honor; that he by the grace of God should taste death for every man."

"I AM ALIVE FOR EVERMORE!"

Here is the second of these two great wonders. First, that the living One was dead; and second, that He is alive forevermore. Christ is the only One of whom that can be spoken. He is the only One who from all eternity lived and once died and is alive forevermore. When we write and speak of any other great world character, all that we can say is that he was born in such a year, and in such a year he died. But when you speak of Christ, you speak of Him as the ever-living One who was born into this world, who died on the cross, who rose again from the dead, and who liveth forevermore. When Festus, the Roman governor, had Paul appear before King Agrippa, who had come on a visit to Caesarea, he explained to Agrippa how Paul had appealed to Caesar, and how he was therefore sending him to Rome; but that he was a little uncertain in his mind as to what to write to Caesar concerning him, and for that reason he wanted Agrippa to examine him. He told Agrippa he had supposed that the Jews had some serious charge against Paul as to certain crimes, but from what he could tell it was a dispute about their own religious views, and "of one Jesus, which was dead, whom Paul affirmed to be alive."

That is the whole issue as to Christ and Christianity. Is He dead or alive? The conviction that He lived, died, and that He is alive forevermore is the conviction which founded the Christian church. That is the belief which sent the apostles forth to preach the Gospel and to greet the flames and the wild beasts with thanksgiving to God and hymns of praise on their lips. A Moslem once boasted to a Christian that his religion had an advantage over the Christian in that the Moslems know the body of Mohammed is in a coffin at Mecca, whereas Christians do not know where the body of Jesus is. And there is just the superiority and glory of the Christian faith! As the evangelist said, "They . . . found not the body." That empty grave is the cradle of the church. We have the record of Jesus' appearance to Mary, to the women, to Peter, to the two on the way to Emmaus, to the ten, to the eleven, to five hundred of the brethren, to the twelve, and last of all, Paul says, "of me also, as of one born out of due time." But Paul was writing long before John wrote, and John might have added to the records of the appearances of Jesus his own testimony, "And last of all, he appeared unto me in glory on the Isle of Patmos." That was the last and final appearance of Christ to one of His apostles. To him that loved Him most Christ granted the vision of the triumphant church and the ever-reigning King.

"AND HAVE THE KEYS OF HELL AND OF DEATH"

The keys were the symbol of authority. When a city was conquered or opened its gate to a conqueror, the leaders of the city delivered over the keys to the conqueror. So Christ holds the keys of the gates of death. Henceforth death is a spoiled kingdom.

The world today is a scene of wild disorder and revolt and rebellion against God. Nevertheless Christian faith knows that Christ is the ruler of the world, and that in the end the whole troubled history of mankind will serve Him, and every knee shall bow of things in heaven and on earth and under the earth, and every tongue confess that Jesus Christ is Lord, to the glory of God the Father.

In one of His exalted moments Jesus said, "I beheld Satan as lightning fall from heaven." Some might say, "I see no signs of that today. I see Satan more firmly established on his throne than ever before, and with more enslaved and fascinated and admiring souls about him than ever before." But that is not the vision of faith, that is not the vision of the one who saw Christ standing in the midst of the seven golden candlesticks and heard Him say, "I . . . have the keys of hell and of death." What John saw is what Christ saw, Satan as lightning fall from heaven.

Death, outside of Christ, is a dread and unconquered kingdom. It is foolish to make light of death. You cannot dismiss it with figures of speech—the "Great Adventure" and that sort of thing. Death is what the Word of God calls it—man's enemy, and the last enemy.

> Death is a fearful thing.
> And shamed life a hateful.
> Ay, but to die, and go we know not where;
> To lie in cold obstruction and to rot;
> This sensible warm motion to become
> A kneaded clod.
> The weariest and most loathed worldly life
> That age, ache, penury, and imprisonment
> Can lay on nature, is a paradise
> To what we fear of death.
> —Shakespeare, *Measure for Measure*

No other conqueror has been able to say, "I have the keys of death!" Alexander, Hannibal, Caesar, Napoleon, all of them had to bow to that conqueror whom we name death. No matter how victorious their armies, they came to a halt on the borders of the empire of death. But death, the great conqueror, has been conquered by Christ. Those few instances in which He showed his power over death—when He said to the ruler's daughter, "Damsel, I say to thee, arise," to the widow of Nain's son, "Young man, I say unto thee, arise," and to Lazarus, three days in his grave, "Lazarus, come forth"—are the prediction and prophecy and example of Christ's complete and final victory over death. "Yes," but one asks, "do men not still die, believer and unbeliever? Do the processions not still wind through our streets on the way to the cemeteries? How, then, can you say that Christ has abolished death and opened its gates?" That is the very thing that He has done. In this present order, in this present dispensation, men still die. But for those who have followed Christ in this life and have fallen asleep in Christ, death has lost its sting, and the grave has been robbed of its victory. "Our Savior Jesus Christ . . . hath abolished death, and hath brought life and immortality to light through the gospel." Of all the accounts of the resurrection of Jesus, I like best that statement in Matthew's narrative where he says that "the angel of the Lord descended from heaven, and came and rolled back the stone from the door, and sat upon it." What a picture that is of death's dominion done for, of death conquered! He rolled back death's stone, and sat upon it!

Christ has the key of death. Think of all that death has done to the world—the antiquity of its reign, the unchallenged sweep of its universal decree and dominion. Then how magnificent is this word of Christ, "I . . . have the keys of hell and death." The Greeks had their own legend of the Sphinx, that monstrous chimera with the face of a woman, the feet and tail of a lion, and the wings of a bird, and who, crouching by the wayside, propounded to every traveler her riddle, and when they could not guess the riddle, their life was forfeited. At length Oedipus guessed the riddle, and in chagrin and anger the Sphinx flung herself down from her mountain cliff and perished. Like the Sphinx of that ancient legend, cruel and inscrutable, death has crouched where the ways of life pass and propounded her riddle, and generation after generation of travelers on the path of life, unable to solve it, have perished. Not the wisest sage or philosopher, no patriarch or prophet, poet or apostle, could solve the riddle. But one day came Christ, He that liveth and was dead, and behold, is alive forevermore, and death's riddle was solved. "O death, where is thy sting? O grave, where is thy victory?" "Thanks be to God, which giveth us the victory through our Lord Jesus Christ."

The conclusion to all this is Christ's "Fear not!" He puts it at the beginning of this great text, but His "Fear not!" is the real conclusion to it. Because these things are true, therefore He says, "Fear not!" How those words "Fear not" ring like a trumpet through the Bible! "Fear not, Abraham"; "Fear not, Moses"; "Fear not, Joshua"; "Fear not, David"; "Fear not, O Israel"; "Fear not, Daniel"; "Fear not, Mary"; "Fear not, Jairus"; "Fear not, Paul"; "Fear not, John."

Many are the things that men fear. Some fear life, lest its struggle and labor be in vain. Some fear sin and temptation, lest it should scar them and destroy them. Some fear poverty, one of the degrading fears of old age. Some fear loneliness. Some fear old age. Some fear the victory of vice and wickedness and unbelief in the world. Some fear, all fear, the last enemy, which is death. But today rings the voice of a risen triumphant Christ saying, "Fear not; I am the first and the last: I am he that liveth, and was dead; and behold, I am alive for evermore."

Those, then, are the great words for all who follow and trust Christ and are faithful to Him—"Fear not!" But not to those who do not own Him, or love Him, or serve Him, who follow afar off, who hide their discipleship in the world, who have neglected and dishonored His church, whose lives are unworthy of their profession, and who are living willingly in transgressions and sin. Not to them does Christ say, "Fear not!" What He says to them is "Fear!" "Repent!" But to all who obey His word, to all who trust in His redeeming blood, to all who love His appearing and Kingdom, Jesus says what He said to John there on Patmos, "Fear not!" He says what He said to the women that morning as He met them as they were coming through the lifting mists, "All hail! All hail!"

10

WHY TARRIEST THOU?

"And now, why tarriest thou? Arise, and be baptized, and wash away thy sins, calling on the name of the Lord." (Acts 22:16)

That seems a strange question to have been addressed to a man like Paul, who was the embodiment of energy, conviction, and decision. Whatever he did, he did with all his might. He never impresses one as a man who hesitates or halts between two opinions. But since this question was asked him, and asked him by God through His messenger, Ananias, it would appear that after his extraordinary experience at the Gates of Damascus, where he was smitten to the ground by the heavenly light and heard a voice speaking to him, "Saul, Saul, why persecutest thou me?" and learned that that voice was the voice of Jesus and in obedience to Jesus had gone into Damascus and had taken refuge in the home of Judas, who lived on the street called Straight, Paul was still delaying to act upon the knowledge that had been given him from the sacred impulse he had felt and had not yet confessed the name of Jesus. At all events, at the direction of God a man named Ananias came to call on Paul at the house of Judas.

When he came to the house of Judas, Ananias, conquering the natural fears that he felt at meeting this bloody persecutor of the Christians, put his hand on him and said, "Brother Saul, receive thy sight." When his eyes were opened, Ananias said to him, "The God of our fathers hath chosen thee, that thou shouldest know his will, and see that Just One, and shouldest hear the voice of his mouth. For thou shalt be his witness unto all men of what thou hast seen and heard. And now why tarriest thou? Arise, and be baptized, and wash away thy sins, calling on the name of the Lord." Then Paul no longer tarried. He confessed his faith in that Jesus whom hitherto he had persecuted and blasphemed, was baptized into the faith of Christ, and went forth to preach His everlasting Gospel.

Wherever the Bible speaks to an individual, it has an accent which speaks to the individual soul in every day and generation. The question which was addressed here to Saul of Tarsus, and in answering which Saul became Paul, is one which speaks to all of us. It tells us the necessity of promptness in action when the voice of God speaks to our souls.

THE VOICE WHICH CALLS US TO LEAVE SIN

"Why tarriest thou?" Here is a question which speaks to every man who is in a wrong way or in the grip of an evil habit. If he knows it to be evil and dangerous, and conscience, or fear, or his better nature has spoken to his soul, telling him to come out of this evil way and to break the chains of this evil habit, then the strange thing is that a man should tarry. Yet nothing could be more apparent than that men do tarry. They delay to make the move, to take the step that will deliver them and set them free.

The longer they delay, the longer they tarry, the harder it will be for them to act. Sometimes conscience and experience point a man to a difficult path. If he is to be delivered out of his present situation, he must take this hard course, and because it is hard often he tarries and delays to take it just because he shrinks from doing that which is difficult, even when he knows the welfare of his own soul is involved.

When the judgment upon Sodom and Gomorrah was just at hand and the heavens were darkening with the imminent doom and Lot had been warned to flee the place with his wife and daughters, even though his sons-in-law refused to go and mocked at him, Lot still lingered. He still tarried. Perhaps he was reluctant, even at the last moment, to abandon all the possessions and wealth that he had accumulated in Sodom, and there Lot would have perished with the rest had it not been that the Lord was merciful unto him, and the two men who were angels laid hold upon his hand and brought him by force out of the city. How could Lot linger, you might say, when he saw the doom coming down upon the city? But that was not more strange than the way in which people linger and tarry today when it has been made clear to them that their present situation has in it all the elements of danger. The longer a man lingers, the longer the chain of habit which winds itself about him. A noted surgeon, performing a most delicate and difficult and critical operation in an operating pavilion in the presence of a class of medical students, after he had finished, turned to the class and said, "Gentlemen, two years ago a simple operation might have removed this trouble and cured this disease. Six years ago a right way of living would have rendered it unnecessary. We have done the best that we can; but now nature will have her way. She does not always consent to the repeal of her capital sentences." The next day the patient died. He was a victim of delay.

THE VOICE WHICH CALLS US TO DO A GOOD DEED

"Why tarriest thou?" Again, this is a question which is spoken to the man who has felt within his heart a desire to do some good deed. Nothing is finer than that. Nothing speaks to the soul so kindly or thrillingly or sweetly as the voice which calls upon it to arise and do some courageous, noble, and generous deed. Is there anyone who has not felt that fine impulse, an impulse which at the time seemed to banish and drive away from his life all mean and selfish thought? Yet how often we hear that voice and do not act upon it. If all who have heard the voice of God calling them to arise and do some noble deed had responded, how different their lives would be today, and how different the lives of others, and how different the life of the world. Perhaps it was a voice that called you to show some sympathy or kindness to one in great sorrow or trial. Perhaps it was a voice that called you to succor the helpless. Perhaps it was a voice like that which the prophet heard,

"Run, speak to that young man. Warn him of the danger he is in and urge him to take another path." Perhaps it was a voice which urged you to speak the word of encouragement to some discouraged or disheartened soul. Why did you linger? Was it because you said you were afraid you would meet with a rebuff? Was it because you felt that you would not be able to speak the right word? Or, as is so often the case, was it because you said, "Yes, I will do it; but I will do it tomorrow?" But before tomorrow came, the one for whom you were going to do it was forever beyond the reach of your ministry.

> So, on our souls the visions rise
>   Of that fair life we never led;
> They flash a splendour past our eyes,
>   We start and they are fled;
> They pass and leave us with blank gaze,
> Resigned to our ignoble days.
> —Sir William Watson, "The Fugitive Ideal"

"Why tarriest thou?" The three disciples, Peter, James, and John, had been asked to watch with Jesus in His agony. I have no doubt that they intended to do so, but they permitted sleep to overtake them; and when Jesus came the third time and found them sleeping, He said to them, "Sleep on now, and take your rest."

What I have just said is profoundly true as to our friends and loved ones. If there is any ministry you think ought to be done them, now is the time to do it. When Judas and the other disciples found fault with Mary because of her beautiful and costly gift, the ointment which she poured on the feet of Jesus, and said that the money ought to have been expended in behalf of the poor, Jesus answered, "The poor always ye have with you; but me ye have not always." In the close and tender relationships of life that is forever true. The generality of people to whom you can show Christian charity are ever about you; but there is that limited number, perhaps just one, of whom it must be said, or who will say to you, "Me ye have not always with you."

THE VOICE WHICH BIDS US COME TO CHRIST

The question was addressed to a man who in a most remarkable way had been invited to come to Jesus, but for some reason hesitated and tarried. Paul might have said, "I must not be in a hurry. I have been in a highly emotional state, and I must test the feelings and impulses which have come to me by the passage of time. If next week or next month, I feel the same as I do today, then I will come to Christ." Or, he might have said, "I will wait till I get back to Jerusalem. I will talk with some of the leaders of the people. I will look back over the experiences I have had at Damascus and then come to a decision." But instead of that, in answer to the appeal of Ananias, "Why tarriest thou?" which perhaps meant only that there was no reason to wait longer, Saul arose. The scales fell from his eyes, and he was baptized and went forth to preach and to live and to die for Christ. He was obedient to the heavenly vision.

"Why tarriest thou?" Not perhaps in the same spectacular and extraordinary way, but nevertheless in reality, the same voice speaks to men today and says to them, "Why tarriest thou? Why do you delay to come to Christ and receive His forgiveness and His blessing?" Sometimes the reason they tarry is because they fear that if they become Christians and come into the church they will have to give up some of the things of the world, some of the things they have been doing. That indeed may be so. But Christ never asks us to give up anything that is for our good. The only thing that He asks us to give up when we come to Him is that which hurts our soul. In the parable of the great supper the master of the feast sent out messengers to invite men to the supper. The invitation of Christ to come to Him and to His church is not an invitation to a funeral. It is an invitation to a banquet, to a supper, to a feast. It is an invitation to taste the highest joys and those pleasures which are forevermore.

Others hesitate and tarry because they say there are things in the Bible which they cannot understand and cannot accept. But these things are never those portions of the Bible which tell us of Christ and His redeeming love. It may be some question, some passage, dealing with history or the creation or the future. Those questions can wait. There is enough in the Bible that is plain and straightforward and unmistakable, which tells us of sin, of life, of destiny, of God, and of the cross, and of the love of God, and of eternal salvation. Those are the things upon which to act. On the walls of Canterbury Cathedral there is a tablet on which is the record of a conversation between Matthew and Prudence in *Pilgrim's Progress* about the Bible:

Prudence: "What do you think of the Bible?"
Matthew: "It is the holy Word of God."
Prudence: "Is there nothing written therein but what you understand?"
Matthew: "Yes, a great deal."
Prudence: "What do you do when you meet with places therein that you do not understand?"
Matthew: "I think God is wiser than I. I pray also that He will please to let me know all therein that He knows will be for my good."

Again, men tarry and hesitate to come to Christ because they say they haven't sufficient feeling. They do not feel themselves great enough sinners. They do not feel the love toward Christ that they think they ought to feel. But there is no place in the Bible which tells us that the time for us to come to Christ is when we feel like it or that we are saved by our feelings. We need to come to Christ because we are sinners and He is the only Savior. Others say they don't feel fit to come to Christ. That is the best reason for coming. The only fitness that we can ever have is to feel our need of Christ and our own unworthiness.

But the common excuse is, "I want to wait. Not yet. I am not ready." But it is always an uncertain and dangerous thing to wait. It is dangerous because the impulse which you have to come to Christ at one time may not move you or stir you ever again. It is always dangerous to say "tomorrow," because tomorrow you may have no desire to come to Christ, although your need will be just as great. It is always dangerous to say you will wait, to say "tomorrow," because you are never sure that tomorrow will ever come. When the Spartans invaded Thebes, Philidas invited them to a banquet. At this banquet, when they were well heated with wine, Philidas had a group of Theban courtesans and beauties brought in to entertain the Spartan chiefs. Just as this entertainment was about to start, the leader of the Spartan chiefs was handed a letter. In the letter was a warning against a plot to destroy him and his companions. But the Spartan leader said to the man who gave him the letter and who told him that it was important, "This is no time for business. Business tomorrow. On with the banquet!" But before tomorrow came, Pleopidas and his fellow conspirators struck their blow and all the Spartans perished. They perished because they said "tomorrow."

It used to be a strange and curious custom in England to put an hourglass in a coffin when it was lowered into the grave. The idea, no doubt, was to signify that for the dead man time was over. But the place where the hourglass ought to be set is not by the side of the dead, for the dead need no counsel, but by the side of the living. God has made great promises of pardon and forgiveness to those who repent and come unto Him. But there is one thing that God has never promised, and that is a tomorrow. Since this is so, if you are one who needs to come to Christ, then "Why tarriest thou?" Do what Paul did when he heard that voice. Arise, and go to Christ!

A young woman who had been asked to come to Christ once said to the celebrated Dr. Chalmers, "I want to wait. I don't wish to accept Christ just now." Chalmers said to her, "Do you wish to wait a year, and not have an opportunity, under any circumstances, no matter what comes up, to accept Christ for a whole year?" She replied, "No, I would not." Then he said, "Do you want to wait a month without an opportunity of coming to Christ?" She replied, "No, I might die before a month was over." "Do you want to wait a week?" "No." "Do you want to wait twenty-four hours?" "No." "Then why not come to Christ now?"

No one who says "I want to wait" would dare to put a definite period to the time he wants to wait, a day, a week, a month, or a year. He would feel that would not be safe. Why, then, tarriest thou? The time to come to Christ is now. Now is the acceptable time. If Christ is the One altogether lovely, the rose of Sharon and the lily of the valley, the chiefest among ten thousand, why wait, why tarry to enjoy His friendship and fellowship? One day with Him will be as a thousand years, and a thousand years as one day. What the converted slave dealer John Newton said about the joys of heaven is true now, even now, of the heavenly life with Christ:

> When we've been there ten thousand years,
>   Bright shining as the sun,
> We've no less days to sing His praise
>   Than when we first begun.

The sooner you begin to sing God's praise, as the One who has redeemed you in Christ, the better it will be for you, and the greater and longer will your joy be.

11

CAN THE ETHIOPIAN CHANGE HIS SKIN?

"Can the Ethiopian change his skin, or the leopard his spots?" (Jeremiah 13:23)

Can the Ethiopian change his skin? Here is the story of one who did. High noon on the desert near Gaza, the gateway to Egypt. To the east and to the south, the undulating sand of the desert; to the west, sand dunes heaped up by the wind; and beyond these hills of sand, the Mediterranean, as blue as the sapphire stone which gleamed upon the breastplate of the high priest. Where the road from Samaria joins the great highway from Mesopotamia to Egypt, there stands a solitary traveler. Looking to the north he decries a cloud of dust. The cloud of dust rolls nearer and nearer, until out of it appear horses and a chariot. The short necks and the narrow heads of the horses declare their Arabian breed, and the decorations on the chariot show it to be a chariot of state. In this chariot sits a black man reading a book. Now the solitary traveler knows why the angel of the Lord has sent him into this desert place. The man and his opportunity are face-to-face.

Long ago, in the time of the prophet Jeremiah, this question was asked, "Can the Ethiopian change his skin, or the leopard his spots?" The question was asked as an emphatic way of expressing the impossibility of a man changing his own ways and his own heart. But here we have an Ethiopian who did change his skin and changed his heart. The story of his conversion naturally divides itself into four parts: first, the preacher; second, the congregation; third, the sermon; and fourth, the results of the sermon.

THE PREACHER

The preacher was Philip, called "The Evangelist." Just as Paul won the title "The Apostle," so Philip seems to have won, by his extraordinary and successful evangelistic efforts, the title "The Evangelist." He was one of the seven men of good report, full of the spirit and of wisdom, chosen by the church at Jerusalem to administer the charities, and care for the widows and orphans and the poor. He remained in Jerusalem, engaged in this pious undertaking, until the time of the great persecution which arose after the death of Stephen and in which Saul of Tarsus was the moving spirit, for he made havoc of the church, entering into every house and hauling men and women to prison. But the blood of the martyr has ever been the seed of the church. Little did Saul and his confederates imagine that when they were stoning Stephen and making havoc of the church at Jerusalem, they were only scattering the Gospel elsewhere, for we read in the Acts that "they that were scattered abroad went every where preaching the Word." So it has ever been. When the mob shot Lovejoy and threw his printing press into the Mississippi River in 1832, all that they succeeded in doing was to set in revolution a thousand other printing presses, whose every revolution helped to sound the death knell of slavery.

Philip quickly showed that he was more than a distributor of charity and became a great preacher of the Word. Before he was taken up into heaven, Jesus had said to his disciples, "Ye shall be witnesses unto me, both in Jerusalem, and in all Judea, and in Samaria, and unto the uttermost part of the earth." And this was the very order in which the Gospel spread. It had been preached in Jerusalem, where it was still supposed that the Gospel was intended only for those of the house of Israel. But Philip went down to Samaria and preached the Gospel where Christ Himself on a memorable occasion had preached

it to the woman of Samaria. Although partly related to the
Jews, the Samaritans were rigidly excluded from the privileges
of Jewish religion. We have hardly any word in our speech
today, or any expression, which could bring out the same degree of scorn and contempt which is brought out in that phrase
of the Gospels, "And he was a Samaritan." Yet it was to these
despised Samaritans that Philip preached the everlasting Gospel. He preached Christ unto them, and, as always where Christ
is truly preached and truly received, there was great joy in that
city. Yet among those who professed conversion and were baptized was the sorcerer Simon Magus, who thought Christianity
was just a new form of magic art and tried to persuade Peter
and John to give him the Holy Spirit for money. It was to him
that Peter said, "Thy money perish with thee." Do not be
disturbed when an impostor or a hypocrite appears in the Christian congregation. He has been there from the beginning and,
I suppose, will be there till the end. Simon Magus, the impostor, was in the gall of bitterness. But there were hundreds of
other lives in Samaria which rejoiced in the Gospel.

In the midst of this successful and moving ministry in
Samaria, Philip was directed by the angel of the Lord to leave
the city and go towards the south in the road to Gaza, which is
desert. This reference to Gaza is one of the many incidental
statements of the Bible which establish the credibility of its
records. The Acts of the Apostles is a book which deals with
one of the most difficult of historical periods because of the
swift changes of local administration, and yet never once, although he mentions so many cities and districts and provinces
and magistrates, rulers, and authorities is Luke found in error.
Gaza was a great city in the Philistine Confederacy. It was
there that Sampson carried off the gates of the city and there,
at the Temple of Ashdod, the blind hero bowed himself and
buried the Philistine lords in the ruins of their temple. Gaza
was taken by Alexander the Great after the battle of Issus and
remained a city of importance until almost the Christian era,
when it was destroyed. But in the first century before Christ a
new Roman Gaza was built, probably not far from the site of
the old city. The old city, which stood two miles in from the
sea on the main highway from Mesopotamia to Egypt, was at

this time, as the book of Acts describes it, a desert. Thus in this brief verse we have not only an accurate historical reference, but also an instance of the fulfillment of a prophecy made centuries before, for in the prophecy of Zephaniah, it was written: "Gaza shall be forsaken, and Ashkelon a desolation." When Philip went down to Gaza, Gaza was desolate and Ashkelon forsaken.

THE CONGREGATION

Some of the greatest sermons have been preached to a congregation of one: Paul's sermon which made Felix tremble; the sermon of Jesus to Nicodemus, in which we have that great statement of conversion and the new birth, "Verily, verily, I say unto thee, Except a man be born again, he cannot see the kingdom of God"; the sermon also which our Lord preached with a well for His pulpit and the much-married woman of Samaria for His congregation. Philip had preached to the crowds in Samaria, but now he is taken away from that popular preaching and is directed to preach to one man. Religion, after all, is individual. We meet together in congregations and say we are all here in the presence of God to hear what God will say; yet, ultimately, religion is a matter between each one of us and God. Life too in all its phases is individual.

> Why should we faint and fear to live alone,
>   Since all alone, so Heaven has will'd, we die?
> Nor even the tenderest heart, and next our own,
>   Knows half the reasons why we smile and sigh.
>
> Each in his hidden sphere of joy or woe
>   Our hermit spirits dwell, and range apart,
> Our eyes see all around in gloom or glow—
>   Hues of their own, fresh borrow'd from the heart.
>   —John Keble, *The Christian Year*

As Philip goes along the lonely highway towards the south, with the sand dunes and the groves of ancient olive trees between him and the Mediterranean, and perhaps wondering why God had called him into this desert place, he is overtaken by a chariot in which is traveling down to Africa a man of Ethiopia, the treasurer of the court of Candace, Queen of the Ethiopians. Candace, like Pharaoh, was the name of a dynasty rather than the name of a person; and here again Luke is shown the exact historian, because ancient writers like Pliny mention this dynasty of female rulers.

The Ethiopian had been at Jerusalem to worship and to attend the feast. This lets us know that he was a proselyte of the gate, the name given to converts to Judaism. As Philip draws near to him, he hears him reading aloud. There was nothing strange about that because there are still parts of the country in which men, when they read, read aloud. I have traveled across the continent and across the ocean many times. But rarely have I seen anybody on a railway car or on the deck of a steamer reading a Bible. I have seen priests and nuns at the appointed hour going through their devotions, as they are required to do, but the ordinary Protestant would be greatly embarrassed to be discovered reading his Bible or a book of devotion in such a public place. Strange comment on our religion.

This Ethiopian, however, was reading the Bible. Sometimes converts to their religion are more zealous than those who have been born in it. It was not easy to read a Bible, or rather a scroll of the Old Testament, closely written in long hand and in difficult script, when one was standing in a swaying chariot as it rumbled along over the rough desert road. Hearing him read and catching a few phrases which let him know that he was reading from the fifty-third chapter of Isaiah, Philip asked him if he understood what he was reading. To us that has a note of impertinence and rudeness. But with Philip it was a natural and courteous expression of interest and sympathy for a man who was reading in a book and in a religion not altogether familiar to him. The Ethiopian answered, "How can I, except some man should guide me?" Then he asked Philip to come up and sit by his side in the chariot. There you can see them, and what a picture for the brush of imagination—the weary but finely bred Arabian horses drawing the chariot, no doubt decorated with the royal insignia of Ethiopia, along the desert highway; a slave standing against the front board holding the lines, and behind him the Ethiopian pouring over Isaiah's sacred page; and at his side Philip, eagerly explaining to him what he was reading. There you have the preacher and the congregation, the chariot for a pulpit, and the undulating desert and the blue Mediterranean for the church building.

THE TEXT AND THE SERMON

The portion of Isaiah which the Ethiopian was reading was that great chapter in Isaiah where the sufferings of our Lord are described, and these verses in particular: "He was led as a sheep to the slaughter; and like a lamb dumb before his shearer, so opened he not his mouth." No doubt when he was at Jerusalem, the Ethiopian had heard the new interpretation which the Christians were giving to this prophecy of Isaiah, declaring that the crucified Jesus whom they followed was the Lamb of God who had been slain, and that this was He who was to be numbered with the transgressors and bear the sins of many and make intercession for the transgressors. It may be too that at Jerusalem the Ethiopian had witnessed the miracle of Pentecost and heard men from all parts of the world speak so that every one could understand them. At all events, he is engaged in reading this marvelous prophecy of Christ.

It was not difficult now for Philip to select the text for his sermon. What greater text could any preacher have than that glorious portrait, the greatest painting in the gallery of the Old Testament. The greatest preacher of all, the Lord Jesus Christ, took it for His text in the same night in which He was betrayed, for He said, after holding the portrait up before His disciples, "This that is written must yet be accomplished in me; and he was reckoned among the transgressors." Beginning at the same scripture, Philip opened his mouth and preached Jesus unto him. How I would like to have heard that sermon! If Philip ran through in his preaching that whole wonderful passage, then he must have told the Ethiopian of how Jesus was despised and rejected of men, how He was wounded and smitten on the cross, how He was numbered with transgressors, crucified between two thieves, how He was buried in a rich man's grave, how He had risen again and appeared unto His disciples, and how this humiliated, bleeding, wounded, and crucified Jesus was nevertheless the exalted Son of God, who one day would come in glory to judge the world and receive His saints.

Why will men preach on something else and something less, when they can speak of Jesus and His cross? Passing a church some Sundays ago, I saw an illuminated sign in front of it with this notice: "Moving Pictures Tonight." As I passed the church, I thought of the immense gulf of distance, both as to chronology, geography, and religion, which stretched between the church and that preaching and this church in the desert where Philip preached Jesus to the black Ethiopian. Years ago there was a preacher in Italy who, in contrast with many of his order in that part of the world at that time, preached nothing but Christ to the people of his town. Having served his day and generation, he fell asleep. But the tradition of his preaching remained long after even his name had been forgotten, and there came a day when the people of this town desired to erect a monument to this priest of whom they had heard their ancestors speak so highly. The monument was erected, a monument without a name, because his name had been forgotten, but on the monument was this inscription: "He Preached Christ unto Us." All other preaching passes and is forgotten. The preaching of Christ remains. The immortal preacher is the preacher who proclaims Jesus Christ the sinner's Savior, the same yesterday, today, and forever.

THE RESULTS OF THE SERMON

When John Bunyan set out from the City of Destruction to go to the Celestial City, he was met on the way by Evangelist, who gave him a roll which was to be his guide to the City of Life. We all need evangelists to help us and direct us on our way to eternal life. Philip played that part to the Ethiopian and played it so well that the Ethiopian became convinced that the one described in Isaiah's passage was Jesus and that Jesus was the Son of God.

The chariot happening to pass a place where there was water; the Ethiopian asked if he might not be baptized. The

Ethiopian wanted to confess his faith and to subscribe to all the requirements of the religion which he was to embrace. Before Philip baptized him he required him, as the church today still does, to make a formal confession and declaration of his faith. He said to him, "If thou believest with all thine heart, thou mayest be baptized." Then he put to the Ethiopian the great question about Jesus Christ, and the Ethiopian made the great answer, "I believe that Jesus Christ is the Son of God." The slave then drew in his horses, the chariot halted, and going down into the water, Philip baptized him in the name of the Father, the Son, and the Holy Ghost.

Jesus told his disciples to go into all the world, saying, "He that believeth and is baptized shall be saved." The Apostle Peter on the day of Pentecost said to the people, "Repent, and be baptized every one of you, In the name of Jesus Christ for the remission of sins." And Paul said, "If thou shalt confess with thy mouth the Lord Jesus, and shalt believe in thine heart that God hath raised him from the dead, thou shalt be saved. For with the heart man believeth unto righteousness; and with the mouth confession is made unto salvation." The great principle which Paul declares and the plan of salvation which he preaches is perfectly illustrated in the conversion of the Ethiopian. With his heart he believed that Jesus was the Son of God. With his mouth he confessed to Philip that faith and then was baptized. Only the Lord knoweth them that are His. But if we can be sure that any man has been saved, we can be sure that this Ethiopian treasurer is now singing the praises of Christ with all the redeemed about the throne of that crucified Lamb of God, concerning whom he had read first in the prophecy of Isaiah, not understanding then who was meant, but the meaning of which was made clear to him by the preaching of Philip.

When they were come up out of the water, Philip went his way and the eunuch his way, but then with a new heart and a new joy welling up out of that heart. He was going back to Africa to administer the finances of the queen of Ethiopia; but now he had become the possessor of a greater treasure than all the treasures of all the kingdoms of all the world. He went on his way rejoicing.

Nothing is said about the joy and rejoicing of Philip. But it was hardly less, if any, than the joy of the Ethiopian. Philip's joy was the joy of Christ who saves the lost. Let us never forget that joy. John Bunyan in his preaching said that the one object of it was the salvation of the souls who heard him. "Oh, these words," he would cry out, "Oh, these words! 'He which converteth the sinner from the error of his way shall save a soul from death.'" God grant that there shall be among us both the joy of conversion and the joy of him whose preaching has converted a sinner from the error of his ways and saved a soul from death.

12

LORD, IS IT I?

"And as they did eat, he said, Verily I say unto you, that one of you
shall betray me. And they were exceeding sorrowful, and began
every one of them to say unto him, Lord, is it I?" (Matthew 26:21–22)

Early on that memorable Thursday, Jesus had sent Peter and John into the city from Bethany to make ready for the celebration of the Passover. He told them that as soon as they entered the city, they would meet a man bearing a pitcher of water. They were to follow him to the house and, going in, were to say to the master of the house, "The Master saith, Where is the guestchamber, where I shall eat the passover with my disciples?" It is possible that this man was a secret disciple. At all events, as soon as Peter and John entered the city, they met the man bearing a waterpot and followed him to his master's house. There they asked the owner of the house what Jesus had told them, and he showed them a large upper room, furnished and ready.

Late that evening Jesus and His disciples bade farewell to beloved Lazarus and his sisters, Mary and Martha, and, leaving the quiet haven of Bethany for the last time, made their way through the shadows of the night into Jerusalem. When they reached the appointed house, they went up the outside stone stairway and entered the large upper chamber which had been prepared for them. The candles were softly glowing on the table, where were displayed the sacred elements of the ancient feast—the roasted lamb, the unleavened bread, the bitter herbs, and the cup of wine.

All over Jerusalem that night lights were glowing in the houses as the families gathered to celebrate the feast of the Passover which had been instituted two thousand years before. As they kept the Passover, they recalled that great night in Israel's history when the angel of the Lord, who smote the first-born of Egypt, passed over the homes of the Israelites where the blood of the slain lamb had been sprinkled on the lintel and the doorposts. At the midnight hour, when all over Egypt there was silence and slumber, within every Jewish home the family stood by the table where the roasted lamb was displayed, their staffs in their hands, their loins girt about them, their shoes on their feet. Not a word was spoken. Then, suddenly, came the signal for which they had been waiting—a great wail of woe, a tidal wave of lamentation that swept over the land, as the Egyptians, from Pharaoh in his red stone palace to the peasant in his cottage and the priest in the temple of Isis and Osiris, awoke to learn that their first-born had been smitten in death. That was the signal for which Israel had been waiting. After four hundred years of bondage the hour of deliverance had struck. Israel started on the Exodus. Israel was on the march, a march that will never end until the world has been redeemed.

Jesus took His place on the couch at the center of the table. After all had been seated, He rose from the table, and, taking a basin and girding Himself with a towel, He went around the table and washed, one by one, the feet of the disciples, even the feet of protesting Peter, and even the feet of treacherous Judas. What a subject that for the painter! Jesus washing the feet of Judas!

When He had given the disciples that great lesson in humility and brotherly love and that marvelous definition of greatness and distinction, Jesus resumed His place at the table. Peter probably was next to Him on His right; John on the other side, for we know that he was near enough to lean on His breast; and ranged along the table on either side of Jesus are the rest of the disciples: James, Andrew, Thomas, Philip, Matthew, and all the others, and Judas with his hand on the bag.

With a troubled look on His face and with a sad accent Jesus said to the disciples, "Verily I say unto you, that one of you shall betray me." At that they were "exceeding sorrowful." On every face but one there was a look of astonishment and grief, every face but one—the traitor's. In the silence, after the words of Jesus were spoken, you could almost hear the beating of every heart, every heart save one—the heart of Judas. After the first shock of amazement and surprise, the silence was broken as the disciples said one by one to Jesus, "Lord, is it I?" Peter, no doubt, was the first to speak, and in his voice there must have been the note of denial, as if to say that for him at least such a thing was impossible. Then the other disciples, one by one, asked the question, "Lord, is it I?" Even John, who looked up from his refuge on the breast of Christ, and even Judas with his hand on the bag and who well knew who it was, asked, "Lord, is it I?"

This question, and this incident, one of the most memorable and moving of all that transpired at the Lord's Supper, tells us of the possibility of evil within our hearts, of our deep ignorance of ourselves, and hence the necessity and wisdom of self-examination.

THE POSSIBILITY OF EVIL WITHIN OUR HEARTS

Jesus said to the disciples, "One of you shall betray me." He knew who it was who should betray Him. Why then did He foretell the betrayal in this vague and general way? Perhaps—who knows?—it may have been a last appeal to Judas to repent before it was too late. But perhaps He left it vague that each disciple might search his own heart. And that is what they did. Jesus said "one of you," and they wondered which one, for they were all men of like passions, and what one of them might do any other might do.

Their question "Lord, is it I?" showed that they realized the oneness of human nature and their common liability to temptation. Hence they did not ask about their fellow disciples, but each one asked for himself, "Is it I?" James did not say, "Thomas is the only one I ever heard express a doubt as to the final triumph of Christ. Perhaps he is the traitor." Peter did not say,

"I have always had my doubts about the sincerity of that publican Matthew and wondered if he left the gains of extortion for nothing." John did not say, "I have been watching how Judas handles that bag, and for some time I have had my suspicions that he is a thief. If there is a traitor among us, he is the man." No! Each man probed his own heart, felt his own pulse, and said, "Lord, is it I?"

There are several ways in which the possibility of evil in our nature is brought home to us. One is when we see or hear or read about transgression in other lives. No matter how far the act seems to be removed from the territory of our own thought and desire, it gives pause for anxious thought and solemn self-scrutiny when we reflect that this was the deed of a man of like nature with ourselves and that all those motives and desires and inclinations which led him to the commission of such a sin lie within our own breasts. The identities of human nature are more significant than their surface differences.

Another fact which teaches us the possibility of evil within our heart is our own experience with temptation. The temptation may have been immediately resisted and rejected. Such a thing may have seemed altogether contrary to our training, our heredity, our experience. Yet the humbling and alarming reflection is that temptation did stop in our path, and it did whisper its invitation in our ear, and thus it recognized a certain affinity with our nature.

When He warned Peter of the temptation which would come upon him, Jesus said to him, "Simon, Simon, behold, Satan hath desired to have you, that he may sift you as wheat." Our English translation does not bring out the important fact that although Jesus addressed Himself to Simon, the "you" which He uses is in the plural. Peter was not the only one of the Twelve whom Satan desired to have. He was after all of them. Thus Christ speaks to us all and warns us all when He said to Peter, "Satan hath desired to have you, that he may sift you as wheat."

Still another way by which we learn our capacities for evil is the degree in which at any time we have yielded to temptation. It may have been only a moment's relaxation—just a step or two in the wrong direction, just the slightest deviation from the path of rectitude. But that little distance was sufficient to let you know how much farther you might have gone. If a warning had not sounded, if you had not been arrested by a sanctifying memory, if some providential incident had not arisen to divert you, if conscience had not rung a warning bell or flashed its flaming sword before you, where would that journey have ended?

OUR IGNORANCE OF OURSELVES

The question of the disciples that night reminds us of our ignorance not only of our potential evil, what we might do, but of evil present in our hearts. If that night one of the disciples was to betray Jesus, the deed was already accomplished in his heart, for there, first of all, men sin and fall. Hence in genuine alarm each one asked, "Lord, is it I?" It was as if each said, "Is it possible that evil has got hold of me to such an extent that I shall deny my Lord?"

Sin can be strongly entrenched in the heart, and yet the heart be ignorant about it. The dim eye, the shaking arm, the declining strength, the vibrations of pain betray the fact of physical sickness; but there is a strange secrecy and inscrutableness about the way sin works in the human heart. The rapidly flowing stream does not betray its power and speed until it strikes some obstruction. So the presence of sin and its powers are not recognized until they are resisted. No bad character is formed in a moment, and no man falls suddenly, however it may appear to outward observation. Could we know the full history of Judas, we could see how, step by step, from one decline to another, he sank to his terrible transgression.

Once when the western hills were all aflame with the glory of the sinking sun, a man came upon an artist painting at the close of day. He asked him first of all to paint the face of an angel, and lo, when he had finished he saw it was the face of his sainted mother in paradise. Then he asked him to paint the face of a sinner, and lo, when it was done, he saw that the face was his own.

Paint me the face of a sinner!
  A darker shadow crept
Down the hill, and I thought
  The unseen artist wept;
And lo, from a magic of pencil
  A face in a moment had grown,
The sad, white face of a sinner,
  And I knew it for my own.

—August Treadwell

One of the reasons why evil is able to work in this manner is the impairment of that instrument by which we judge, and that is conscience. The more a man sins, the more his conscience declines, and the feebler becomes the sound of its warning voice. Another reason why sin is able to work in secret is the common disinclination to know anything unfavorable concerning ourselves. Every soul has its warnings, and the angel of conscience gets his message through even to the most careless and unwilling heart. In the solicitude of the sick bed, in the narrow escape from death, in the arresting thoughts that come by an open grave, in contact with some pure and lovely character, in the fragment of some prayer or sermon, in the light that streams from the Communion table, in all these ways men are pled with and warned by the Holy Spirit. But too often they turn away from such warning and information and seek to forget in the midst of the world the unpleasant truth that has been learned.

THE WISDOM OF SELF-EXAMINATION

The apostle said, "Let a man examine himself, . . . for he that eateth and drinketh unworthily, eateth and drinketh damnation to himself." That does not mean that a man is to examine himself and discover that he is a saint, but rather that he is to examine himself and discover that he is a sinner and needs that great act of divine mercy and cleansing of which the broken bread and the outpoured cup are the symbols. This is perhaps the greatest blessing of the Lord's Supper to our lives. It draws our thought for a little while away from the world and centers it upon our souls. Everything about this supper is so solemn, so moving, so humbling, that, of necessity, we search our own hearts.

Instead, therefore, of trusting in your own heart, the wise thing to do is to accept the Bible's verdict about your heart when it says that it is deceitful above all else, and he that trusteth in his heart is a fool. Look, then, at your heart through this powerful magnifying glass, the Word of God. Hear the question those disciples asked, "Lord, is it I?" Remember that even Peter, in spite of his shocked protest at the very suggestion of such thing, did that very night deny with an oath that he had ever known Jesus. When you see others fall into sin, when you see others drifting away from Christ and out of His church and bowing down to the idols of this world, pass no quick judgment upon them, but say to yourself, "Lord, is it I?" "Who can understand his errors? Cleanse thou me from secret faults." "Search me, O God, and know my heart."

But if in that question of the disciples, "Lord, is it, I?" there is a solemn warning and an invitation to self-examination, there is also in it a note of hope and cheer. All of them asked that night, "Lord, is it I?" but only one of the Twelve betrayed Him. All the others, in spite of misunderstandings and temporary lapses and falls, were finally and gloriously faithful to Christ and won that noble title given them in the exalted language of the *Te Deum*, the "glorious company of the apostles."

Thus Christ opens to men not only their capacity downward, and shows each man his ladder that leads to hell, but He shows their capacity upward, and their ladder that reaches to heaven. If He warns men from their sins, He also calls them to His service and to His fellowship. Suppose that Jesus that very night had sketched the future of all those disciples—suppose He had told them how James, the brother of John, would stand fast and be the first to win the martyr's crown when he laid down his head on Herod's gory block; suppose He had told them how Peter, in spite of the fall which He predicted for him that night, would repent, be restored, strengthen the faith of his brethren, go out to become the heroic leader of the early church, and win at length the martyr's crown; suppose He had told them how John, leaning there on His breast at the supper, would be the bravest among the apostles, would not love his life unto the death but would suffer banishment and imprisonment on the lonely Isle of Patmos and there would be granted a vision of the future triumph of the church, and that he would write the five books which will guide and comfort the church until Christ shall come again; and suppose He had sketched to us the unknown history of the other eight apostles, what labors they would perform, what churches they would build, and that all the names of the twelve apostles of the Lamb, with only one missing, would be written on the foundation walls of the holy city—suppose He had done that; how each disciple then would have started with joy and wonder and said, "Lord, is it I!"

Would that I had the tongue of an archangel to describe for you your capacity and possibility as a redeemed soul—what you might do and be, in and for the church, what testimony you might make to Christ, what hearts you might comfort, what lives you might bless! Then you would exclaim, not as the disciples did that night, in fear and trembling, but in joy and glad surprise, "Lord, is it I!" When you think of that, when you think of that "I" who is possible in you through Christ Jesus, then will you say as you go to the Communion table, not only "Lord, is it I? Can it be I?" but "Lord, it shall be I!"

13

WHAT DOEST THOU HERE?

"And he came thither unto a cave, and lodged there; and, behold,
the word of the Lord came to him, and he said unto him,
What doest thou here, Elijah?" (1 Kings 19:9)

The devil, according to the legend, once advertised his tools for sale at public auction. When the prospective buyers assembled, there was one oddly-shaped tool which was labeled "Not For Sale." Asked to explain why this was, the devil answered, "I can spare my other tools, but I cannot spare this one. It is the most useful implement that I have. It is called 'Discouragement,' and with it I can work my way into hearts otherwise inaccessible. When I get this tool into a man's heart, the way is open to plant anything there I may desire." The legend embodies sober truth. Discouragement is a dangerous state of mind because it leaves one open to the assault of the enemies of the soul.

Elijah was down and almost out. The last time we saw him was at the moment of his great triumph over the prophets of Baal. The view from Mount Carmel is one of the grandest in all the Holy Land. Looking westward and northward one sees the waves of the Mediterranean breaking in white lines on the shore of the beautiful bay and against the gray walls of Acre, the Ptolemais where Paul landed and the stronghold before whose walls in 1799 Napoleon Bonaparte suffered his first serious reverse. Looking eastward and northward one sees the hills of Nazareth, the great plain of Esdraelon, and the tower-ing mountain of the Transfiguration, Mount Tabor. It was here on the slopes of Carmel that Elijah won his signal victory over the prophets of Baal when the Lord answered him with fire. After the destruction of the prophets of Baal and the coming of abundant rain after the years of drought, Elijah girded his loins and ran before the chariot of King Ahab from Carmel to Jezreel. What a picture! There you have Elijah the very incarnation of victory and triumph.

But now we see him under a juniper tree, asking God to take away his life. What a contrast between the Elijah of Mount Carmel and the Elijah under the juniper tree! What has hap-pened to this great servant of God, in some respects the great-est who appears in the pages of holy writ? When Jezebel, Ahab's queen, heard the news of the slaughter of her favorite prophets, that fierce and strong-minded woman was beside herself with rage: "So let the gods do to me, and more also, if I make not thy life as the life of one of them by tomorrow about this time." After Elijah's heroic and courageous testimony be-fore Ahab and his corrupt court, you do not expect him to be frightened by anything or anyone upon earth. But when Elijah heard the savage threat of Jezebel, he left his post at the court and, apparently without divine sanction or permission, fled for his life into the wilderness, clear down into the desert country about Beersheba. There, faint and exhausted, smitten with the heat and glare of the inexorable sun, Elijah sank down under the juniper tree and asked God to put an end to his life. Elijah did not want to be killed by a wicked woman, but he did want to die. "It is enough," he groaned. "Now, O Lord, take away my life; for I am not better than my fathers."

ELIJAH'S DISCOURAGEMENT

Here we have a man so discouraged that he wants to die. Life has lost for him the interest and the zest of living, of going on. All of us have spent, or will spend, some time under the juniper tree and will know what it means to be discour-aged. The contributory causes are many and different, but the state of mind is the same. It may proceed from a weary, broken, or sick body; from frustrated hopes and ambitions; from waves of affliction which have broken over the soul; from a sense of uselessness and failure; and, most keenly of all, from the knowledge of transgression and sin. Hence, it will be worth our while to pause for a little by the juniper tree and talk with God and Elijah. We are not prophets like Elijah, and we live more than 2,800 years after his day. Yet he was a man, we are told, of like passions with us, and human nature is the same from age to age. That is the fascination and profit of biography, especially biblical biography. When you study these characters, you study your own life.

One of the chief causes of Elijah's discouragement and almost despair was undoubtedly physical. Elijah, although he stood in the presence of God, had a body just like our own. We hear much about the influence of the mind over the body, but this does not displace the fundamental fact that the body has an influence over the mind. Elijah suffered from the reaction of the great encounter and the great triumph on Mount Carmel. The hundred miles and more that he had traveled, from Jezreel to Beersheba, a trying journey under the best conditions even today, was sufficient to break him down and prostrate his body. There is no doubt that this was one of the causes of his distress, because the first thing that the Lord did was to minister to his body. The angel gave him food and drink and then sleep. "So he giveth his beloved sleep." When a man is utterly discouraged and depressed, sleep may be the thing he needs first of all.

> Sleep that knits up the ravelled sleave of care,
> The death of each day's life, sore labour's bath:
> Balm of hurt minds, great nature's second course,
> Chief nourisher in life's feast.
> —Shakespeare, *Macbeth*

The psalmist said, "Thy gentleness hath made me great." The tenderness and gentleness of God is very beautiful here in His dealings with the exhausted and discouraged prophet. The angel came and gave him food and drink, after which Elijah lay down and slept. Then the angel awakened him and again invited him to take food, telling him that the journey he was to take to Horeb was too great for him.

When you are cast down and discouraged, do not forget the body and its necessities. The English physicist Tyndall used to suffer from discouragement and melancholy, due to an oppression in his chest. Then all seemed dark and dismal. But he was careful, he said, to discard any opinions he might have formed during that period of depression. Mariners take their bearings when the sun or the stars are visible. Do not rely upon the estimates and judgments of your discouraged moments. God did not take Elijah's verdict of himself at this moment as the final fact about Elijah. He dismissed the verdict of the moment of despair and recalled Elijah to his better self.

Another cause of Elijah's discouragement was his sense of loneliness. He had stood, as he thought, all alone in his defense of God's truth and in his opposition to the idolatry and corruption of Ahab's court. When you see Elijah standing before the wicked king and pronouncing the judgment of the drought or confronting the four hundred prophets of Baal, you say, "Here is a man who is above the necessity of companionship and sympathy." But such a man never existed. Elijah was a man of like passions with us. The soul reaches out for the sympathy and friendly companionship of others. In its lonely moments it feels that there is no such sympathy or companionship and is tempted to fall down under the juniper tree. "I was lonely," spells the secret, not only of many a discouragement, but of many a breakdown in character which has followed such discouragement.

Then Elijah was disappointed. After the overthrow of the false prophets of Baal, Elijah must have thought the cause of Jehovah would now everywhere be triumphant, and that the apostate court and nation would now return to the Lord. But in this he was disappointed. In a few days he found himself a fugitive in the wilderness of Beersheba, a price set on his head. All his great efforts, he thought, had gone for nothing. That is why he said, "It is enough; now, O Lord, take away my life; for I am not better than my fathers." They could not overthrow idolatry in Israel, neither can I.

But, as the sequel shows, Elijah was mistaken. He was not

so lonely as he had imagined himself to be. His great ministry and testimony had not been in vain, for there were seven thousand in the nation who had not bowed the knee to Baal or kissed him. Elijah had helped to save the nation from complete apostasy and idolatry. In that respect his life had been a tremendous success. Elijah didn't know who or where the seven thousand were. He had not seen them or heard them; but they were there, encouraged in their faith by the testimony and courage of the great prophet. Ministers, Sunday-school teachers, Christian workers, fathers and mothers, interested and self-sacrificing friends sometimes get discouraged about the results of their work. They may feel that their work is as great a failure as Elijah felt his to be when he lay down under the juniper tree. But could we see all that God sees, perhaps our hearts would be uplifted. The best part of your work and influence is unseen. "Cast thy bread upon the waters: for thou shalt find it after many days."

Having ministered to Elijah's body by giving him food and sleep, and having encouraged him by showing that he was not alone and that his labor had not been in vain, the next thing that God did for Elijah was to put him to work. "What doest thou here?" was the question He put to the discouraged prophet. It was no place for Elijah, groaning and complaining under a juniper tree in the desert, when there was work to do for God in the world. Elijah tried to defend himself by relating what he had done in the services of God. But God showed him that that is not enough. There is still work to do. He put Elijah to work again and sent him on his important mission to anoint Jehu to be king over Israel and Elisha to be his successor. It must have been with an altogether different feeling, and with the old flash of light in his eye and the old look of courage and invincibility about him, that Elijah set out on that commission. Now he knew that God's work would go on. When he was gone, Elisha would take his place. Elijah asked God to let him die; but now he learned that it is not Elijah who is to die, but wicked Ahab, whose blood the dogs will lick where they had licked the blood of murdered Naboth, and wicked Jezebel too, whose body, thrown out of her palace window at Jezreel, the dogs would devour.

CURES FOR DISCOURAGEMENT

When cast down and discouraged, one of the best cures is to try to do something worthwhile for others. John Keble used to say, "When you are quite despondent, the best way is to go out and do something fine to somebody." In the thought and act for others we relieve the misery of our own distress. You may not be called upon to anoint prophets or kings who are to hurl other kings from their thrones, but there is always some good that you can do.

The fact that there are so many discouraged people always about us in the world and, I suppose, a greater number just now than ever before affords an opportunity for real helpfulness and soul ministry. How many a man, once in as low a state of mind as Elijah, recalls with deep gratitude the word of counsel, the act of kindness, or the letter of friendship that helped him in that dark hour. At the unveiling of the memorial to his friend and co-laborer Richard Cobden, John Bright related how, when his young wife lay dead in his home and the bottom had dropped out of everything and life was only a dismal blank to him, Cobden came to visit him. Instead of the usual words of condolence, this is what Cobden said: "There are thousands of homes in England today where mothers and little children are dying of hunger because of a famine in bread made by law. Now when the first paroxysm of your grief is past, I advise you to go with me, and we will never rest till the corn laws are repealed." John Bright's great ministry in behalf of the poor of England goes back to that interview with Cobden, when Bright was sitting under the juniper tree.

Few know how great a part General Grant's friends played in his great career. What, for example, his chief of staff John Rawlins, the Galena lawyer, did to keep him from intemperance, or what Sherman did to keep him in the army. After the victories of Fort Henry and Fort Donelson, Grant was shabbily treated by the commanding general Halleck and was virtually under arrest for misconduct. After he was restored to his army, he won the great battle at Shiloh in April, 1862. But after that victory General Halleck himself joined the army, and Grant was reduced to a merely titular command. His position became intolerable, and he determined to resign from the army. He had his effects packed and was about to leave. Sherman came to see him and, sitting down on one of the boxes, expostulated with him and pled with him to reconsider his resolution. There had been a day, he said, when he had felt just the way Grant did, but now all was prosperous with him. He was sure it would be so with Grant if he remained with the army. Some happy event would come along, and everything would be changed. Grant reluctantly agreed to stay in the army. In a few weeks the happy event turned up in the appointment of General Halleck to the chief command at Washington This put Grant at the head of his army again, and the way was opened for him to carve out his great career with ponderous hammer blows at Vicksburg, Chattanooga, Missionary Ridge, the Wilderness, and Appomattox.

There was a time when things were at a low ebb with David. Hunted over the Judean hills by King Saul, David was losing his grip on himself and beginning to lose his faith in God and in his destiny. It was at that time that his best friend Jonathan went out at night to David in the Wood of Ziph and "strengthened his hand in God." Blessed be God for those who in some dark and trying hour have strengthened our hand in God.

The deepest discouragement, I suppose, arises out of the knowledge of our moral failures and transgressions and our sins. When a man realizes how he has sinned against his own soul, when he has been his own worst enemy, when an old besetting sin has tripped him and thrown him, or when he has been tempted into some sad and deplorable act, something that he never thought he would or could do, then the devil is sure to try to tie him hand and foot with the heavy chain of discouragement. The danger then is that a man will say to himself, "It doesn't matter now what I do or what I say. No one cares, anyway. I've gone this far; I might as well go the whole distance." That is the way the devil treats a man in the time of his sin and transgression.

But Christ has a far different method. He lets us know that He cares, that He loves us even to the uttermost, and that He is able to save even to the uttermost. He tells us that we are of such worth, even in our sins, that for the salvation of our souls

He was willing to shed His precious blood on Calvary's cross. That is the view to take of your soul. In the time of discouragement do not take your own estimate of yourself as the true one, but take the estimate of Christ. You are worth the shedding of His precious blood. He does not say, "It is of no use; you can never get up; you might as well go the whole distance." But what He says is this, "Though your sins be as scarlet, they shall be as white as snow."

Margaret Slattery, in her *Living Teachers*, tells of a community in which a stranger came to settle and to engage in the practice of law. He immersed himself in his legal work, and when he was sometimes seen walking at the eventide, he walked alone, with his head down, and with the look of mental distress upon his face. One day he confessed to an artist who had a studio in the town that he had made one sad and terrible mistake in his life. The artist said nothing but parted from him and went into his studio. Weeks afterwards he invited this melancholy and dejected lawyer to come in and view a portrait which he had finished, telling him that it was his masterpiece. The man was surprised and pleased that his judgment should have been sought by the artist, but when he went into the studio to view the portrait, he was surprised to see that it was a portrait of himself, only now he stood erect with his shoulders thrown back and his head up, ambition, desire, and hope written on his face. Regarding it in silence for a few moments, the man said, "If he sees that in me, then I can see it. If he thinks I can be that, then I can be that man; and, what is more, I will be."

14

BARABBAS, OR JESUS?

"When they were gathered together, Pilate said unto them, whom will ye that I release unto you? Barabbas, or Jesus which is called Christ?" (Matthew 27:17)

Down in the lowest cell of the Roman dungeon a manacled prisoner lay on the cold, hard floor. For months he had languished in that dungeon. He had been sentenced to death for robbery, murder, and insurrection, and this was the day set for his crucifixion. In the wall above him was a small opening with iron bars. When morning came, the slightest gleam of light appeared like a shadow at that barred window. Then the prisoner knew that it was day, and when that gleam of light faded, he knew that night had come again. As he lay there looking up at the window, he suddenly heard a sound. Getting up, he grasped with his hands two bars at the window and stood there, alert, listening.

What the prisoner had heard that morning was the most fearful sound that falls upon the human ear. It was the voice of the mob—cruel, wild, animal, devilish, thirsting for the blood of the innocent. That is always the most dreadful of all sounds, the roar of the mob, for man is the only wild animal. "Crucify Him! Crucify Him! Crucify Him!" That was the cry that reached the ear of this prisoner as he stood there holding to the bars of the prison window. The sound came and went like the breaking of the waves of the ocean, a mighty roar, then an interval of silence as the wave receded, and then another crash and roar, "Crucify Him! Crucify Him! Crucify Him!" But between those shouts the prisoner thought he caught the echo of another shout, "Barabbas! Barabbas! Barabbas!" Then again, "Crucify Him! Crucify Him! Crucify Him!" Then once more he caught the word "Barabbas." What could it mean? That was the prisoner's own name! "Fools! Dogs!" he exclaimed. "Don't they know that this is the day I am to be crucified? Why do they shout for it?" Then with a groan of anguish and a muttered curse, the prisoner, to the loud clanking of his fetters, fell back in despair on the floor of his dungeon.

Pontius Pilate was determined to let Jesus go. There was no doubt of that. At least so far—up to the point of not jeopardizing his own comfort and welfare. That determination to let Jesus go was born within the mind of Pilate the moment Jesus was brought before his tribunal. His first expedient was to let the Jews deal with Him themselves. He said in effect, "Ye have a law. Take Him and try Him." But they wanted the blood of Jesus and reminded Pilate that it was not lawful for them to put a man to death. Pilate then took Jesus aside into his chambers and had that memorable interview with Him, at the end of which he brought Him out again before the crowd and said, "I find no fault in Him." But they shouted, "Away with Him, away with Him, crucify Him. . . . He stirreth up the people, teaching throughout all Jewry, beginning from Galilee to this place." Pilate caught at that. If He came from Galilee, then he could turn Him over to the jurisdiction of Herod, who happened to be in Jerusalem at that time. But Herod, after he had mocked Jesus and set Him at naught and clothed Him in a scarlet robe, sent Him back to Pilate.

This time the perplexed Pilate tried a compromise. He said in effect to the accusers of Jesus, the chief priests and the rulers, "I have examined this Man, and have found no fault in Him; neither has Herod, who has sent Him back to me. Nothing worthy of death has been done by Him. I will therefore chastise Him and let Him go." It was the hope of Pilate that if he inflicted upon Jesus the terrible Roman scourging, that would satisfy them. But he had not measured the depth of their hatred. Just at that moment there was an interruption. A crowd of people came before the tribunal asking Pilate to follow the annual custom at the time of the Passover and release unto them a prisoner for whom they might ask. That gave Pilate another chance. He would release Jesus unto them! The people themselves had no fault to find with Jesus. Indeed, one of the reasons why the rulers wanted Him put to death was because He was so popular with the people. This stratagem of Pilate might have succeeded but for an interruption which probably sealed the fate of Jesus. Just at that moment Pilate's wife sent a message saying, "Have thou nothing to do with that just man: for I have suffered many things this day in a dream because of him." Pilate was considering this matter, this message from the world of dreams, still pondering what he should do with Jesus. But while he did so, the chief priests and rulers went among the crowd inciting them to ask for Barabbas.

Barabbas was a robber and a murderer with a long record of crime behind him. He had been apprehended and sentenced to death and was to be crucified that day. Waiting in his cell far below, Barabbas heard the soldiers coming down the corridor and then the key turning in the lock of his cell. "Now," he said to himself, "my hour is come!" The soldiers seized him but, to his surprise, conducted him not to the place of scourging, as the custom was before crucifixion, but to the tribunal of Pilate. There he stood facing the crowd and on the other side of Pilate, the other prisoner.

By a singular coincidence the name of each prisoner was Jesus![1] Barabbas was not a name, but a family description, meaning the son of a rabbi. This son of a rabbi had gone wrong and after years of wickedness and crime was about to pay the penalty for his sins. On the other side of Pilate stood Jesus of Nazareth, the King of the Jews. Rising from his ivory seat, Pilate pointed to the two prisoners and said, "Whom will ye that I release unto you?" The words were hardly out of his mouth before a wild shout shook the fortress and palace and echoed down the narrow streets of Jerusalem, "Barabbas! Barabbas! Barabbas!" Not this man, but Barabbas! "Crucify Him! Crucify Him! Crucify Him!"

Amazed, shocked, angry, and disappointed at the preference

---

1. One of the old manuscripts of the New Testament gives his name as Jesus.

of the priests and the people, Pilate told the soldiers to take Him and scourge Him. In that brutal scourging before crucifixion the prisoner was beaten with a whip at the end of which were balls of iron. When the soldiers had scourged Jesus, they put Herod's mocking robe of crimson on His back and a crown of thorns on His head and brought Him again to the tribunal of Pilate. Pilate was still hoping that the people would change their minds and be satisfied when they saw Jesus scourged and bleeding. "Behold your King!" he cried. But they shouted, "Away with Him, away with Him, crucify Him." Pilate answered, "Shall I crucify your King?" But back came the roar, "We have no king but Caesar!" Then Pilate released unto them Barabbas and delivered Jesus to be crucified.

An Amazing and Shocking Preference

Pilate was shocked and amazed that the priests and the people should have preferred a red-handed robber and murderer to Jesus. As Peter afterwards said to their faces, they "denied the Holy One and the Just, and desired a murderer." To us too it seems incredible that a blood-stained killer should have been preferred to Him who went about doing good, the friend of man. An incredible thing, you say. Yet that choice still echoes today. Still we hear that cry, "Not this man, but Barabbas!" Wherever the world chooses force, violence, greed, hatred, there it asks for Barabbas instead of Jesus. Wherever Jesus as a person, a principle, an institution, a way of life is rejected, there Barabbas is chosen, and there again the cry goes up, "Not this Man, but Barabbas!"

Is Barabbas such a stranger after all? Do we not all have a Barabbas in our own hearts? Have you never heard him shout, "Release me! Crucify Jesus!" Whenever we turn from and refuse Christ and His way of life and His spirit and yield to anger, covetousness, impurity, envy, jealousy, selfishness, hatred, evil speaking, what we have done is to choose Barabbas instead of Jesus—"Not this Man, not His way, not His authority, but Barabbas!"

There comes a time in the life of every soul when the decision which it has made as to Jesus is final and irrevocable. On that day at Pilate's tribunal the crowd was confronted by Jesus Barabbas and Jesus of Nazareth, and they chose Barabbas. They never had an opportunity to withdraw their choice or reverse their decision, for never again did Jesus and Barabbas appear together before them. They asked for Barabbas, demanded the crucifixion of Jesus, and shouted, "His blood be on us." That choice was final. So there comes a time when your decision as to Jesus is final and irrevocable. What is that decision today? Is it for Him or is it against Him? Is it for Jesus or for Barabbas? If you have not decided, remember that not to decide is to decide against Him. Standing by the cross this day, I call upon you to choose life or death, Jesus or Barabbas.

BARABBAS LIVED BECAUSE CHRIST DIED

Barabbas lived because Christ died. If that crowd that day had asked for Jesus instead of Barabbas, then, instead of Jesus being crucified between two thieves, there would have been three thieves hanging on those three crosses, and the one in the middle would have been Barabbas instead of Jesus.

Look at Barabbas, as he stands there by the side of Pilate, with Jesus on the other side. Barabbas could hardly credit his senses as he heard the people shout for his release. The soldiers came up and struck the shackles from his arms and ankles, and giving him a rough push, said, "Get out of here! You are free!" Slowly he walked down the marble steps of the tribunal and passed into the crowd, a free man, amid shouts of rejoicing from the multitude. One of his old gang came up to him and, slapping him on the shoulder, said, "Well met, Barabbas! It's been poor going without a leader. Now we will get back on the job again. Tomorrow a rich caravan from Damascus, bound for Alexandria, will pass between Jericho and the Jordan. After we have done that job, we will go down to Joppa, where a rich Roman centurion, who has three beautiful daughters, has built a castle for himself. That too will bring us a rich harvest. I will get the others together, and we will meet at the Jericho gate tomorrow morning at early cock crowing." But to the bandit's surprise, Barabbas paid no heed to him and walked off in another direction.

Standing on the edge of the crowd, Barabbas watched as Jesus, bleeding from the terrible scourging of the soldiers and with His own seamless robe on His back, was led away with two other criminals, robbers like himself. Barabbas followed the march of death to Golgotha. In front haughtily strode the centurion. On either side were the soldiers, every now and then holding their spears horizontally and pushing the crowd back. Behind the prisoners was another soldier, urging them on with whip and oath. When Barabbas saw Jesus faint and fall beneath His cross—who knows ?—perhaps he had the impulse to hurry forward and take up His cross for Him, for he knew that he was the one who ought to have been bearing that cross. But before he could act, the centurion called on Simon to take up the cross.

In the crowd at Calvary, Barabbas watched as the soldiers nailed Jesus and the two robbers to the three crosses. He saw the crosses upended and then heard the loud chorus of mockery and taunting and blasphemy as the chief priests and the Pharisees and the rulers of the people and the rabble swarmed about the cross, hurling their imprecations and curses in the teeth of Jesus. One of the two thieves, no doubt a member of the same gang as Barabbas, caught sight of him and turned from mocking and taunting Jesus to curse Barabbas, "How did you get those chains off? You are the black-hearted traitor and coward who saved your neck by betraying me and my comrade here to our enemies. You are the one who got us into this fix. But for you we never would have been on this cross. But now we moan and groan and suffer this terrible death, while you, the worst of all, go free! But wait, Barabbas, your day will come; and when it comes may these nails be as sweet to you as they are to us!" And Barabbas himself wondered why he was free.

Standing in the crowd near the cross, Barabbas heard Jesus say, "I thirst!" and he would have liked to quench His thirst for Him. He heard Him say to a man who stood near Him: "Son, behold thy mother." He heard one of the thieves, one of his old comrades in crime, say to Jesus, "Lord, remember me when thou comest into thy kingdom," and then the sublime answer of Jesus, "Today shalt thou be with me in paradise." At the ninth hour he heard Jesus cry with a great voice, "It is finished!" As he groped his way with the people back to Jerusalem in the supernatural darkness, Barabbas said to himself, "He died for me! If He had not died, then I would have died."

Christ died in the place of Barabbas. There is the central and glorious truth of the Cross. Christ died for you and me. He died for the just and the unjust. He died that He might bring us to God. He died that we might not forever die. That, and nothing else, is the eloquent sermon of the Cross.

Of all the men around the cross, Barabbas is the greatest and plainest and most eloquent preacher, for by his escape from the cross he tells us that Christ died that sinners might live. Christ offers you life through His death. Have you accepted that offer? If you have, then are you going His way and living in His spirit? Will the remembrance of His crucifixion bring you nearer to Him and separate you from that world that still shouts for Barabbas and still asks that Jesus be crucified?

Or have you not yet accepted that great love and pardon which Christ on the cross offers to you? Are you just one of the crowd who are watching Him die, like that crowd that stood afar off and watched Him die on that Friday on Golgotha's skull-shaped hill? He came to pay your debt, to set you free from the penalty of sin. Just as truly as His death on the cross that day set Barabbas free, so Christ is able to set you free. Were you there when they crucified your Lord? Yes, you were there. You were all there when they crucified your Lord. It was your sins which nailed Him to the cross. You were there. But will you be there when all the prophets and all the apostles and all the martyrs and that robber who repented and asked Jesus to remember him when He came into His Kingdom and all those who have been redeemed by His blood and saved by His death gather before the throne of God and sing of Him who died for them and for you and for me, "Worthy is the Lamb that was slain to receive power, and riches, and wisdom, and strength, and honor, and glory, and blessing"? Will you be there then?

15

HOW WILT THOU DO IN THE SWELLING OF JORDAN?

"If in the land of peace, wherein thou trustedst, they wearied thee, then how wilt thou do in the swelling of Jordan?" (Jeremiah 12:5)

Since the first river went out of Eden to water the earth, never has there been such a river as the river Jordan. Born in the snows of Hermon not far from Caesarea Philippi, it flows southward and enters the Sea of Galilee, 682 feet beneath the level of the sea. Issuing forth from the Sea of Galilee, it follows a winding, tortuous course, as if striving and struggling to avoid its fate where it enters the waters of the Dead Sea, 1,292 feet below sea level.

Without a parallel in its flow and destiny, the river Jordan, although one of the shortest rivers in the world, little more than two hundred miles in length, is the most historic of all rivers. Standing on its banks, the great memories of the Jordan come back to you. The crossing of the Jordan by Joshua and the people of Israel, when the priests carried the ark of the covenant into the river, and the waters of the river stood up in a wall to the north and flowed away to the south, and the people passed over dry shod. The day when the soldiers of Jephthah held up the fleeing Ephraimites at the fords of the river and put them to the sword when they could not pronounce the difficult word "shibboleth." The day when David crossed the river on a ferry, leaving the body of his beloved Absalom lying under the stone pile in the wood of Ephraim. The day when Naaman, the leper, washed seven times in the Jordan and was cured of his leprosy. The day when John baptized Jesus in the river and then saw the Holy Spirit descend upon Him. The sacred history of the Jordan and the crossing of it by the children of Israel on their way out of Egypt to the land of Canaan made the Jordan from the earliest Christian age a proverb or symbol of the immortal soul of man crossing the river of death at the end of life into the kingdom of heaven.

> Roll, Jordan roll;
> I want to go to heaven when I die,
> To hear sweet Jordan roll.

It was a pleasant summer day when I stood on the banks of the Jordan as it flowed between the thickets and bushes, the branches of the plane trees reflected in its peaceful waters. There was nothing about the stream that day to suggest a great and famous river except its memories. But when I looked up from the river to the trees that border it, there, high up in the topmost branches of the trees, I saw the sticks and the stones, the rubbish, the flotsam and the jetsam which had been deposited by the river when it overflowed its banks. There was the incredible high-water mark of the Jordan; and looking at that high-water mark in the tops of the trees, I thought of this old question in the book of Jeremiah, one of the grand old texts which dropped out of preaching long ago but is ever timely for our souls, "How wilt thou do in the swelling of Jordan?"

The prophet Jeremiah was troubled because of the afflictions which had come upon Jerusalem and the prosperity of the wicked. That is one of the oldest questions, "Why do the wicked prosper?" Job asked it; David asked it; the saints have asked it; and Jeremiah asked it. He wondered at the power and influence of the enemies of Jerusalem, whether foreign foes or her own citizens. Addressing himself to God, he said, "Righteous art thou, O Lord, when I plead with thee: yet let me talk with thee of thy judgments: Wherefore doth the way of the wicked prosper? Wherefore are all they happy that deal very treacherously?"

God has a way of answering questions by asking another question. That was the way He answered Job when Job was troubled by the prosperity of the wicked and his own afflictions. At the end of Job's long series of questions and eloquent appeals, God answered Job out of the whirlwind. He answered him with a series of questions, the purpose of which was to humble Job and bring him to see that if he knew so little about the ways of God in the physical universe, it was not strange that there were providences of God in his life and in God's government of the world which he could not understand. "Where wast thou when I laid the foundations of the earth, . . . when the morning stars sang together, and all the sons of God shouted for joy? or who shut up the sea with doors?. . . Have the gates of death been opened unto thee?. . . Canst thou bind the sweet influences of Pleiades, or loose the bands of Orion?"

And in a like manner God answered Jeremiah's question about the prosperity of the wicked by asking him a question, "If thou hast run with the footmen, and they have wearied thee, then how canst thou contend with horses? and if in the land of peace, wherein thou trustedst, they wearied thee, then how wilt thou do in the swelling of Jordan?" At first that seems no answer to Jeremiah's question. Jeremiah had not asked God to tell him what he—Jeremiah—would do under certain given circumstances, but he wanted to know what God was going to do, and why He permitted men to do what they had done and were doing. Yet there was profound meaning and satisfaction in the answer that God gave.

The answer was in the form of a double metaphor. The first is borrowed from the field of battle—"If thou hast run with the footmen, and they have wearied thee, then how canst thou contend with horses?" If a man has not been able to battle successfully with the infantry, what will he do when he has to fight against the cavalry? The other metaphor is borrowed from a journey. If the traveler has been wearied by the ordinary incidents of his journey, the heat and the fatigue of it, then what will he do when he comes to the river Jordan, when the Jordan overflows its banks? "How wilt thou do in the swelling of Jordan?" It was as if God had said to Jeremiah, "You are troubled now by my government of the world. You are troubled by the liberty given to evildoers and by the events which have transpired in Jerusalem. But what wilt thou do when far worse things happen, when pestilence and famine and death stalk through the streets of the city and the holy place and the holy vessels are profaned, when the people are carried captive into Babylon and thou thyself art carried an unwilling fugitive down into Egypt?"

We have every reason to believe that the question God asked Jeremiah brought him to himself, for in the swelling of the Jordan, when the darker and worse events came to pass, so grandly did he bear witness to God and His righteousness that ages afterwards, when Christ was on earth and one day asked His disciples, "Whom do men say that I am?" they answered that some thought He was one of the great prophets, others that He was mighty Elijah, but still others that He was Jeremiah come back to earth. What a tribute that was to Jeremiah!

This question about the swelling of the Jordan gives expression to the truth of the necessity of overcoming faith for a triumphant passage through life. Whatever difficulties we have known thus far, in comparison with them those to come will be like contending with horses and passing through the swelling of the Jordan.

LIFE'S TRIALS

Life is of the nature of a trial, the purpose of which is to produce moral and spiritual qualities with a view to their complete unfolding and coronation in the life to come. In this trial there are what we might describe as major and minor trials. These minor trials in a way test us and prepare us for the greater trials to come. If in these you have kept your balance and your courage and hope, then you have good reason to expect that you will stand firm when the great trial comes upon you. But if in the time of the smaller trials you have been shaken and troubled or afraid, then how will you do in the swelling of the Jordan, when the great trial comes?

This question was addressed to Jeremiah and through him

to us, not to alarm us or discourage us, but to prepare us and strengthen us for what is to come.

We all have rivers to cross in life. When Lincoln was on his way to Washington to be inaugurated, he stopped for a time in New York. Everybody then was asking, "Are we to have a civil war?" This is the way Lincoln answered the question: One night when he was a circuit-riding lawyer in Illinois, he stopped when darkness fell at a log tavern. Staying over night in the same tavern was a circuit-riding Methodist preacher. The lawyers were wondering about the Fox River and whether they would be able to ford it. They gathered about the circuit-riding preacher and asked him what he thought. "Oh, yes," he answered, "I know all about the Fox River. I have crossed it often and understand it well, but I have one fixed rule with regard to Fox River—I never cross it till I reach it." Not to cross rivers until you reach them may be good advice, for a lot of people in their worries cross rivers before they come to them. But the fact is that there are many deep and wide and swollen rivers to cross in life, and the wise man will make what preparation he can in advance.

Temptation is one of the rivers of life that we have to cross. It is a river which flows across every man's path. Temptation is one of the chief trials of life. Indeed the two words are almost synonymous. But there are different degrees and kinds of temptation. If in some of the lesser temptations we have failed, what are we going to do when the great temptation comes down upon us? If some little slight or disrespect or annoyance has made you angry and you lost your temper, then what are you going to do when you suffer some real affront or are the victim of some real injustice? If in patience, thoughtfulness, generosity, absolute frankness and sincerity, or in our speech concerning others through lack of vigilance and lack of faith we have failed, then what are we going to do when some great temptation seeks us out—a continuing irritation, such as made Moses smite the rock twice and shut him out from the Promised Land; or a sunset look at a woman upon a house-top, such as brought God-loving and God-praising David down into the dust as an adulterer and a murderer; or a moment's fear of injury to ourselves or our interests, such as made warm-hearted, loving Peter declare with an oath that he had never known his Lord? Then indeed we shall need the help—and thank God we can have His help—of the Captain of our Salvation, who has said, "Greater is he that is in you, than he that is in the world."

Sickness is one of the trials of life. If you have languished and been broken in spirit because of a few poignant pangs of pain or a few days or a few weeks of invalidism, then what are you going to do when real and prolonged sickness and suffering come upon you, and you are shut up a prisoner in your room and at evening say, "Would God it were morning!" and at morning sigh, "Would God it were evening"? Then you will need—and thank God you can have—the strength and help of Him who said to Paul of his thorn in the flesh, "My grace is sufficient for thee: for my strength is made perfect in weakness."

Sorrow is another of the rivers of life we have to cross. If, when you have lost some of your money or a piece of property or a friend upon whom you counted lifted up his heel against you or some long-cherished ambition vanished forever over the horizon of life, if these things vexed you and troubled you and grieved you and perhaps even made you question the way of God with man, then what are you going to do when some great sorrow comes sweeping down upon you? When God separates you from one who is the "desire of your heart," the apple of your eye, the light of your daily life, leaves you only the memory of an all-too-brief happiness, when that comes upon you, when you hear the roar and sweep of those waters, then what are you going to do? Ah, then you will need—and thank God you can have—the presence and the comfort of Him who said, "When thou passest through the waters, I will be with thee; and through the rivers, they shall not overflow thee."

Conscience is another of the trials of life. Strange, mysterious, indefinable, inescapable, august conscience! If, in the busy arena of this life, conscience has sometimes been able to draw you out of the crowd and bring you into a corner by yourself, if in spite of all the pleasures and occupations and business of life which divert or engage or amuse you here, conscience has been able to give you an unpleasant and bitter moment, then how will it be in the great day when you stand before the judgment seat of Christ, and every word that you have spoken comes back, and every deed and every secret thought is flashed before you, then what will you do when there is no business, no occupation, no pleasures to divert you or to turn aside the accusation of conscience, as in this life? Oh, in that hour you will need—and thank God you can have—the protection and refuge of your Redeemer and Advocate who comes to take your place, in whom, long ago, you put your trust, and concerning whom you can say, "I . . . am persuaded that he is able to keep that which I have committed unto him against that day."

THE FINAL TRIAL

At length, at the end of the journey, comes the final trial. As we have seen, Christian thought and devotion for many ages has taken the crossing of the Jordan at a time when it overflowed all its banks as a proverb and sign of the soul's crossing of the river of death. No matter how we keep silent about that last event in life, we must all meet it. One by one we come down to the banks of the river Jordan where

> Death like a narrow stream divides
> That heavenly land from ours.
>
> —Isaac Watts

Yes, there it rolls and there it flows, that river that lies between this land and that other country! If in the ordinary experiences of life you have been troubled, then what are you going to do when you come down to this river?

When Christian and Hopeful at the end of their pilgrimage came down to the river and saw how deep and wide and swift and dark its waters were, they were stunned. They met two men whose raiment shone like gold and their faces as the light, and they asked them if there was no other way to get to the gate of the heavenly city except by going through the river. Were there no boats, bridges, fords, or ferries? But the two men said, "You must go through, or you cannot come at the gate." Then they asked the men if the waters were all of one depth? They answered, and here is one of the greatest things in *Pilgrim's Progress*, "You shall find it deeper or shallower as you believe in the King of the place."

Then they went down into the river. Christian began to sink and cried out, "All His waves go over me." But Hopeful answered, "Be of good cheer, my brother; I feel the bottom, and it is good." With that Christian broke out with a loud voice, "Oh, I see Him again; and he tells me, 'When thou passest through the waters, I will be with thee; and through the rivers, they shall not overflow thee.'" Then they both took courage, and the enemy was after that as "still as a stone, until they were gone over." Remember what the two men with the shining faces said to the Pilgrims, "You shall find it deeper or shallower as you believe in the King of the place."

A few days before she received her summons, a mother whom I had visited from time to time said to her daughter, "I have been thinking about a text that I heard my minister preach on in Scotland when I was a girl."

"And what was it, Mother?" asked the daughter.

"It was something about horses and the swelling of the Jordan. Yes; that's it. 'If thou hast run with the footmen, and they have wearied thee, then how canst thou contend with horses? and if in the land of peace, wherein thou trustedst, they wearied thee, then how wilt thou do in the swelling of Jordan?'"

"What a strange text!" said the daughter. "What could the minister ever get out of that text?"

"What," said the mother in her soft Scottish voice, "what could the minister get out of that text? What could he get out of it but this: that when we take our friends, our father or our mother, brother or sister or little child down to the river, that is as far as we can go with them. We cannot go into the river with them, and when we ourselves go down to the river, that is as far as they can go with us. Then it is you and your Savior for it."

"You and your Savior for it." Yes, that is it! In the great trials of life and in life's final and supreme trial, that is it—"You and your Savior for it." Can you count on His help in that hour? Why travel alone when you can have a companion like that. "How wilt thou do in the swelling of Jordan?" Not the person across from you in church, not your friend or neighbor, not your father or mother, your brother or sister, but thou! How wilt *thou* do? Will you have to do it alone? Or will you have that Friend who never leaves you and never forsakes you, that Friend who has said, "Lo, I am with you alway even unto the end of the world," and who, having loved you, will love you to the end?

16

HOW CAN MAN BE JUSTIFIED WITH GOD?

"How then can man be justified with God?" (Job 25:4)

"Being justified by faith, we have peace with God." (Romans 5:1)

The Bible asks some questions which are hard to answer, and which, were it not for the Bible itself, would never have been answered. The question asked here by Bildad of his friend Job is fundamental. The Bible has a way of sweeping aside the nonessential and getting at once to the root of the matter. Most men who have thought at all about the life and destiny of man have agreed that man's chief end and happiness consists in enjoying the presence and the blessing of God. Most agree too that something has happened which interferes with that natural fellowship and communion with God. There need be no quarrel about the how and why. We look now at facts: man is unjust, God is just; man is unrighteous, God is righteous. It would be absurd to speak of getting by this difficulty by a change in the nature and person of God. The very name of God carries with it the idea of unchangeableness. With Him there is no shadow of turning. Whatever change there is to be must be wrought in man. The unjust must be made just, and the unrighteous must be made righteous. Thus we come back to the question of the text: "How can man be justified with God?" To put the matter in a way that shall not savor of textbooks or outworn terms, let us suppose that a man dies and goes to heaven, which means simply to a full enjoyment of the presence of God. How did he go to heaven? Why was he admitted to be with God? In answering this we shall answer the other question: "How can a man be justified with God?" Here are some of the answers:

BY NATURAL RIGHT AND INHERITANCE

A man goes to heaven for the simple reason that he is a man and inherits all the possibilities of the human life. The heavenly life is the last stage in the development of man, and man passes into heaven by the same right that he passes from infancy to childhood and from childhood to manhood. Man deserves acceptance with God just as he deserves the privilege of breathing the air which is necessary for his physical life. God created me, therefore I claim all that God can give to any other man. Stripped of its philosophy and poetry, this is the doctrine of the universalist. All men are saved because they are saved. But this position, aside from the flat contradictions of Scripture, that flesh and blood cannot inherit the Kingdom of God, will not satisfy the objections of our reason. You can't put yourself in Chicago by saying that you are going there or that you have a right to be there; neither am I satisfied that I shall get to heaven because I want to go or feel that I have a right to be there. Before I am satisfied in my mind that I shall reach Chicago, I must be convinced that there is a railroad running thither and that it is constructed with the purpose and power of carrying just such a person as myself. In the like manner, before you convince me that I shall get to heaven, I must know how. My belief is founded on knowledge. This is the query of the text, "How can man be justified with God?" To say that a man goes to heaven because he is a man gives me no answer as to the "how."

BY SUPERIORITY OF CHARACTER

This man agrees that to send all men to heaven as they *are* would only reproduce the conditions of this world and that heaven would be simply this world on a larger and more durable scale. Only those will go to heaven who deserve to go. And when you ask him who deserves to go, he replies that that must be determined by character. In this world we speak of good character and bad character. Only those who have a good character will be justified and admitted to heaven. Character, by men, cannot always be determined. Our means of knowledge are so incomplete and fallible. But God, the all-knowing and the all-seeing, would labor under no such difficulty. Who knows the heart? 'Tis He alone. Because He is God He knows just how good or how bad a man's character is. With this knowledge He will justify only those who are good—who have righteousness. We can all think of lives at the opposite poles of morality. A saintly, godly Christian mother, whose eyes wait for the coming of the King and whose thoughts dwell ever in the shining country, would readily be set apart as one of those who is fit for heaven; whereas a criminal, stained with all crime and infamy, would readily be classified among the unfit. But as we come back from these two extremes of morality, it becomes more and more difficult to establish a dividing line and to determine when a man is on the side of acceptability and when he is on the side of rejection. No one, not the most gifted among the sons of men, would want the task of picking out that number among men who are fit for heaven. Yet if a man gets to heaven by character, that choice must be made by someone. We cannot do it, but perhaps God, with His infinite wisdom, can do it. Yet, even granting that God could or would choose out for salvation those men who had reached a certain standard of character, would this be a reasonable, or even just, method of procedure? Suppose that the passing scale were 90 per cent. Then the man who got as high as 89 per cent would be shut out of heaven, although between him and the man who was admitted there was just one per cent of difference in character. That offends our sense of justice. If one man is to be saved and another man lost, we feel that tremendous difference in destiny demands a tremendous difference in character, not a slight hairbreadth difference in virtue. Salvation by personal character, instead of being the natural and reasonable method, is unreasonable and unjust. It is far better that no effort be made to distinguish at all and that men as men be admitted to heaven. Furthermore, if I am to be saved because I have attained a certain degree of excellence in character, how will I ever know whether or not I have reached that passing point? Only the day of final destiny would reveal it, and until then, instead of having a fearless assurance of salvation, I must wait in unrest and anxiety. The further we go into this answer, that a man shall become just with God by his own character, the deeper is our perplexity and the more unsurmountable the difficulties.

BY THE FREE PARDON OF GOD

The man who makes this answer speaks very much like a Christian and may sincerely think himself to be one—and may even be one. He confesses that men are not going to heaven by right of birth and that so far as character is concerned, none of them is fit for heaven or can become justified, for righteousness or perfection must be the basis of the justification. Man's sin and unrighteousness stands between him and heaven or justification with God. But God in His mercy pardons our iniquity through Jesus Christ. But does that make me just and hence fit for heaven? I may be pardoned, but is a pardoned man a just man? Or an innocent man? The governor might pardon a man who is in jail. The man comes out free and with all the privileges of his fellow citizens. But that pardon did not make him a good man, and it did not make him an innocent man. He merely escapes some of the punishments imposed upon the criminal. The sinner must be pardoned before he gets into heaven; but that is not all, nor is it the transaction or the change which fits him for heaven and the fellowship of God. To say then that a man gets to heaven because his sins are pardoned would be equivalent to saying that a thief or a murderer becomes a good citizen because the clemency of the governor has saved him from the gallows. We have still found no answer to the all-important question: "How can man be justified with God?"

THROUGH FAITH IN CHRIST

We have laid hold upon every means of justification which man might use and have found each in its turn useless and unavailing. But the extremity of man is the opportunity of God. By finding that man cannot justify himself, we have reached the greater discovery that someone outside of man must do it. We were right when we said that the standard of acceptability with God must be established by God Himself. And God has established that standard—nothing short of righteousness. "Be ye holy for I am holy." Blessed are the pure, not half-pure, almost pure, but the pure in heart, for they shall see God. His law convicts everybody and takes away all vain hope of making ourselves acceptable in His sight. To be justified with God we must be worthy of justification, that is, we must satisfy the demands of God. I must be righteous, if not of myself, then by another; and that other is God. The best of men and of saints, who, of all men, might have had a right to put forward their own character, have been the first to confess their total unfitness and unworthiness and to subscribe themselves the chief of sinners. If that was their feeling in the matter, what then shall we say of the great number of men? It was not necessary that man should be justified, desirable and blessed as that condition might be. An unjust man does not deserve justification; but if any can justify him, it must be God. Here we come to the great answer of Christianity: "It is God that justifieth!" Upon that rock Christ builds His church, and the gates of hell cannot prevail against it.

The Grounds and Means of Justification

The ground of our acceptance with God is the acceptability of Christ. Since I could not supply righteousness, someone else had to supply it if I was to be justified. Christ has supplied that righteousness. He and I exchange places. He takes my sins and I take His righteousness, and I am accepted in the Beloved, that is, in Christ. "The justification of man is the divine acquittal of man for the Son of man's sake."

How do I secure this great gift, the righteousness of Christ? God does not thrust it upon men indiscriminately or against their wish. But he offers it freely to all; I receive it through faith. My faith is the appropriating act whereby I secure the righteousness of Christ, which is the gift of eternal life. Being justified by faith, we have peace with God through the Lord Jesus Christ. The source, the wardrobe where the white robe of justification is found is Christ Jesus; the hand by which I take the garment is my faith.

How then can a man be justified with God? By faith in the Lord Jesus Christ. What shall I do to be saved? Believe on the Lord Jesus Christ, and thou shalt be saved! Christianity is not an emotion, the expression and the power of tender and benevolent sentiments. It is not knowledge; it is not obedience; it is not devotion to a great example. It is faith in the Lord Jesus as the One who by His cross and resurrection secures to man acceptance with God. Christians might differ as to modes of baptism, or even about the manifestation of the divine in the human life of Jesus, and still be one in faith. But the cross of Christ separates into a hopeless division. Either Christ justifies me with God, or He does not. I must take Him as a Savior, or I must leave Him. I may keep Him as an example, an inspiration, a guide to life's vexed ways, but I have lost Him as Redeemer and Savior. Surely then differences of attitude here, faith or unbelief, are not minor differences. If a man can devise some other way of being justified with God, let us have it. If he cannot, then is he a wise man who neglects so great a salvation?

But have you ever heard of a man who rejected Christ as Savior because he had discovered some other means of justification with God? They have rejected Him without providing some other way. May these plain words recall to Christian believers the true object of their faith, and to those who have not yet said, "I believe," and are secretly trusting in their own merit and works, may these words be used of God to tell them that outside of Christ no man can be accepted of God.

In the present crisis in the Christian church, and with an enmity and opposition to the Gospel in the world almost unsurpassed in the ages, the supreme duty of the church and of the faithful minister of Christ is to keep plain and clear before the church and the world what God has done in Christ for our salvation. If the knowledge of that, if love and wonder and awe at it, should ever fade from the church and from the minds and hearts of professing Christians, then woe to the church. A true understanding of Christ's work as a redeemer from sin, and a love for Him as the One who loved us in His death on the cross is the Christian believer's refuge from the temptations and the dangers of this world, his inspiration to a godly life, and the ground of his hope for eternal life. He who keeps close to the cross will keep close to the Christ who died upon that cross.

On one of the old churches of Germany there is cut in the stone the figure of a lamb. That monument has an unusual history. The one who placed the lamb there as a memorial was a workman who, once employed at work on the roof of the church, fell from the roof and would have been killed had not his fall been broken by a lamb which was grazing on the sward of the churchyard. The man's life was saved, but the lamb was killed. In gratitude to God for sparing his life, the workman had the figure of the lamb cut into the stone in the wall of the church.

The Lamb of God, our Lord Jesus Christ, who taketh away the sins of the world, is the One who, by His love and sacrificial death, broke our fall and saved us from that death which is the penalty upon sin. Are you resting upon that Lamb of God?

17

MY GOD, WHY HAST THOU FORSAKEN ME?

"And about the ninth hour Jesus cried with a loud voice, saying, . . . My God, my God, why hast thou forsaken me?" (Matthew 27:46)

The religion of Benjamin Franklin, as outlined by his statements and his published creed, was far different from that of the evangelical church. Nevertheless, when Benjamin Franklin came to die, he directed that a crucifix, or a picture of Christ on the cross, should be so placed in his bedroom that he could look, as he said, "upon the form of the Silent Sufferer." When we read that incident, we conclude that he was not far from the Kingdom of Heaven. It is when we center our thoughts and our gaze upon Christ on the cross that we come to the heart and power and glory of the Christian faith.

Of the Seven Words from the cross, this is the only word recorded in the first two Gospels, Matthew and Mark. The fact that these two writers record this prayer of Jesus is a strong testimony to the authenticity and credibility of the Gospels; for had the Gospels been the work of some forger, he surely would have omitted such a prayer as this, in which Christ confesses, or seems to confess, that God has forsaken Him, for such a confession would be out of keeping with the claims of the hero and with the works elsewhere attributed to Him.

From the sixth hour until the ninth hour there was darkness

138

over the face of the earth. This is a darkness that no science can explain. It was not the darkness of night, for it came on at twelve o'clock and lasted until three. Nor was it the darkness of an eclipse, for the moon was at its full. It was nature's great expostulation and protest against the crucifixion of her Lord and Maker.

> Well might the sun in darkness hide,
>   And shut his glories in,
> When He, the mighty Maker, died
>   For man the creature's sin.
>
> —Isaac Watts

This period of darkness from the sixth hour until the ninth seems to have been also a period of silence. None of the Seven Words from the cross belongs to this period of darkness. But at the ninth hour Jesus broke the silence with his cry, "My God, my God, why hast thou forsaken me?"

Because of the similarity in sound between "Eli" and "Elijas" or "Elias," some of those who stood by thought that He was crying for Elijah. Incidently, this was a great tribute to that mighty prophet. It was Elijah who had been summoned up out of the unseen world to talk with Christ about the cross and the Atonement, when with Moses he appeared in glory on the Mount of Transfiguration. If anyone out of the Old Testament could have helped Christ in this hour, Elijah was the man. In the hours of stress and danger when the storms break over us, not the easygoing, easy-principled men are the ones who help us, but men of iron and granite, men of storm and struggle, men of tremendous conviction like the prophet Elijah.

It was not Elijah for whom Christ was asking or to whom He was crying, but Elijah's God. "My God, my God, why hast thou forsaken me?" What was back of that cry? Had the incidents which had taken place at the cross, such as casting dice for His garments and offering Him vinegar to drink, recalled to Christ Psalm 22? Was He just softly repeating to Himself that psalm, and His words became audible when He reached that verse, "My God, my God, why hast thou forsaken me?" Or was it the natural shrinking of the soul and the body from death? Or was it that, for a little, the union between the soul of Christ and God was broken? Or was it that on the cross Christ was vicariously bearing the wrath of God upon sin? We instinctively shrink from a too curious effort to analyze the inner feelings of our Lord in this tragic hour. Where no answer is given, perhaps we ought not to attempt to answer. Nevertheless, generally speaking, there are just two positions which we can take with regard to this cry: Christ was mistaken or He was forsaken.

CHRIST WAS MISTAKEN

Many helpful comments and sermons have been constructed on the theory that Christ was mistaken. The six hours and more of suffering on the cross had weakened Him so that His mind temporarily collapsed and His spirit drooped and flagged, and in His weakness He thought that God Himself had forsaken Him. He was not really forsaken, but He *thought* that He had been forsaken.

In this respect the case of Jesus would be analogous to that of Elijah, who one day ran in triumph before the chariot of Ahab and called upon God to vindicate himself by fire, and the next fell beneath the juniper tree and prayed for God to take away his life, "It is enough; now, O Lord, take away my life; for I am not better than my fathers." His case would also be similar to that of John the Baptist, one day standing before Herod and Herodias and denouncing them for their adultery and saying to Herod, "It is not lawful for thee to have her," but when he had been cast into prison for that brave sermon, sending out of the prison that message of doubt and depression and gloom to Jesus, "Art thou he that should come, or look we for another?" In the last hours of Martin Luther and John Knox we have an echo of this same feeling of depression. If this is all there was in the experience of Christ, that He only *thought* He was forsaken of God, then it is quite in keeping with what is frequently observed in some of the greatest men, a period of intense faith followed by a feeling of God-forsakenness and abandonment.

But such a view will never be acceptable to those who hold

high thoughts of the person of Jesus. I am reluctant to think that our Lord Jesus Christ in the most important hour of His life was the victim of a false impression and gave expression to that false impression. If this is a saying of Jesus which was founded on a misunderstanding and afterwards had to be withdrawn, then it is unique and peculiar among the utterances of Jesus. If He had been only a great saint or martyr, we might understand it. It would not interfere with our admiration for His character. But in spite of what ideas we might hold about His limitation during the days of His incarnation, to think that in the Son of God, in this the greatest hour of His life there was this misapprehension and misunderstanding is to reduce Christ in rank and in glory. Therefore we dismiss it.

CHRIST WAS FORSAKEN

If Christ was not mistaken when He made this cry, then He was indeed forsaken. Whatever the reason for His being forsaken, there is no question as to the fact. This experience of severance from God marked the climax of His suffering. This was the bitterness of His cup. He had experienced suffering and humiliation and pain of all sorts, but never when they scourged Him and buffeted Him and mocked Him, gave Him sour vinegar to drink, pressed the crown of thorns upon His brow and drove the nails through His flesh, did Jesus say, "Why, my God, hast Thou done this?" But now in the ninth hour, His lips are opened and He cried, "My God, my God, why hast thou forsaken me?" In all His other trials, in the battle with the cup in Gethsemane, He had assurance of His Father's presence. Angels were there to minister to Him; but on Calvary the Father's face was veiled.

The speedy death of Christ was probably the result of this desolating sense of God's absence. Pilate was amazed when it was reported to him that the prisoner was already dead when the soldiers came to break the thighs so that the body could be taken down before the Sabbath. Christ did not die of exhaustion; He cried out, not in poor, weak, faltering tones, but with a loud voice just before His death: "My God, my God, why hast thou forsaken me?" If there had been a doctor's certificate or a coroner's verdict given, it would have been this: "Died of a broken heart."

Why was He forsaken? We must remember that only Christ had the right to ask such a question. Even interpreting it in the sense of the ordinary hard experiences in life, Christ alone was forsaken in that He drank the cup of sin. But only Christ had the right to ask "Why?" It is not strange that God should forsake any of us, but Christ His eternal Son, who perfectly did His will—why?

This abandonment by God was the sinner's penalty. The penalty upon sin is death—death, spiritual separation from God. This, as tasted by Christ, was the utmost price of the world's redemption. For the sake of all sinners Christ was made a curse, and with the burden of the world's woe upon Him, He passed out into the lonely darkness.

It is only upon this ground that you can explain the strange shrinking of Christ from His death and the pain and humiliation of it. If it was only from a physical death, if it was only from mental and spiritual humiliation and suffering from which Christ was shrinking, then we would have to agree with Celsus, and many a scoffer since, that martyrs at the stake, and even criminals, have met death in a more courageous way. But if Christ was shrinking from the utmost penalty of sin—the darkness of separation from God—then I can understand His bitter prayer in Gethsemane, "If it be possible, let this cup pass from me." I can understand the blood drips which distilled upon His brow, and if it was from this terrible doom that He was drawing back, then I can understand His cry, "My God, my God, why hast thou forsaken me?" That mysterious, indefinable, indescribable something which is the penalty upon sin Christ was meeting. He was drinking in the darkness our cup.

That this was the price of our redemption, that this was the work of atonement, shows the awfulness of sin. If any man thinks lightly of sin or thinks that sin can be remedied by some light, cheap method, let him hear the echo of that cry from Calvary, "My God, my God, why hast thou forsaken me?" That cry is the measure of God's wrath towards sin; it is the measure of God's love for man; and the measure of Christ's work for our redemption. Christ is able to save unto the uttermost them who come unto Him because He Himself in the work of atonement went unto the uttermost. He suffered for us without the camp.

This cry is our hope, and we have no other hope. When Christ cried out, "My God, my God, why hast thou forsaken me?" the price of our redemption was paid. This cry is our comfort. It is no special comfort for me to know that Christ too was thirsty, that Christ suffered loneliness, that Christ thought God had forsaken Him. But there is great comfort in the knowledge that upon the cross Christ passed through utter desolation, experienced the utmost penalty of sin, separation from God, in order that you and I might never despair, that we might never be forsaken.

> Yea, once Immanuel's orphan cry His universe hath shaken—
> It went up single, echoless, "My God, I am forsaken!"
>
> It went up from the Holy lips, amid His lost creation,
> That, of the lost, no son should use those words of desolation.
> —Elizabeth Barrett Browning, *Cowper's Grave*

18

IF A MAN DIE, SHALL
HE LIVE AGAIN?

"If a man die, shall he live again?" (Job 14:14)

The famous Russian author Ivan Turgenev, at the end of his great book *Fathers and Sons*, describes a village grave-yard in one of the remote corners of Russia. Among the many neglected graves there was one untouched by man, untrampled by beasts. Only the birds rested upon it and sang at daybreak. An iron railing ran around it. Two fir trees were planted at each end of the plot. In this grave was buried the brilliant but wayward son of the country doctor Bazaroe. Often from the nearby village two feeble old people, husband and wife, moving with heavy steps and supporting one another, came to visit this grave. Kneeling down at the railing and gazing intently at the dumb stone under which their son was lying, they yearned and wept. After a brief word they wiped the dust away from the stone, set straight a branch of a fir tree, and then began to pray. In this spot they seemed to be nearer to their son and to their memories of him.

And then Turgenev asks:

> Can it be that their prayers, their tears are fruitless? Can it be that love, sacred, devoted love, is not all powerful? Oh, no; however passionate sinning and rebellious the heart hidden in

the tomb, the flowers growing over it peep serenely at us with their innocent eyes. They tell us not of eternal peace alone, of that great peace of indifferent nature; they tell us, too, of eternal reconciliation and of life without end.

A beautiful tribute, that, to a father's and mother's love for a son who had passed into the unseen, and a noble expression of the hope of "eternal reconciliation and of life without end." But upon what is that hope based?

THREE ANSWERS

"If a man die, shall he live again?" As to the first part of that question, there is no doubt. There is no "if" about it. "It is appointed unto men once to die." The question is "Shall he live again?" This is man's greatest and most earnest question.

> One question more than all others
>> From thoughtful minds implores reply;
> It is as breathed from star and pall,
>> What fate awaits us when we die?

The first answer comes from the materialists, those who say all there is to man is bone and flesh and blood. They answer the question as to what happens after death by saying, "Nothing happens. Where do we go? We go nowhere. Earth to earth, ashes to ashes, dust to dust. That is the end of us. The soul is but a function of the brain." "Knock me on the head," said Napoleon, "and where then is my soul?"

A second answer is that of science. But the lips of science are sealed. The answer of science is best stated in the words of a very great scientist, Dr. William Osler, late professor of medicine at Oxford:

> Whether across death's threshold we step from life to life, or whether we go whence we shall not return, even to the land of darkness, as darkness itself, the scientist cannot tell. Nor is this strange. Science is organized knowledge, and knowledge is of the things we see. Now the things that are

seen are temporal. Of the things that are unseen science knows nothing, and has at present no means of knowing anything.

A third answer is that of the agnostic. That is a word which was invented by Thomas Huxley. It is a transliteration of the Greek word which means "unknown," and which Paul saw on that altar to the unknown god in Athens. The agnostic does not say, out and out, that there is no future life, but rather that we cannot know whether there is or not. If you leave out the divine revelation, that, of course, is so. The classic expression of agnosticism was that eloquent address delivered by Robert G. Ingersoll at the grave of a child:

> Why should we fear that which will come to all that is? We cannot tell. We do not know which is the greatest blessing, life or death. We cannot say death is not good. We do not know whether the grave is the end of life, or the door of another, or whether the night here is not a dawn somewhere else. Neither can we tell which is the more fortunate, the child dying in its mother's arms before its lips have learned to form a word, or he who journeys all the length of life's uneven road, painfully taking the last slow steps with staff and crutch. Every cradle asks us, "Whence?" and every coffin, "Whither?" The poor barbarian, weeping above his dead, can answer these questions as intelligently and satisfactorily as the robed priest of the most authentic creed. The tearful ignorance of the one is just as consoling as the learned and unmeaning words of the other.

CHRIST'S ANSWER

The fourth answer is that of Christ. About to be separated from His disciples by death, He said to them, "Let not your heart be troubled: ye believe in God, believe also in me. In my Father's house are many mansions; if it were not so, I would have told you. I go to prepare a place for you. And if I go and prepare a place for you, I will come again, and receive you unto myself; that where I am, there ye may be also."

This great answer of Christ tells us that beyond death

> There is a land of pure delight
>   Where saints immortal reign;
> Infinite day excludes the night,
>   And pleasures banish pain.

—Isaac Watts

The reality of this life to come is based by Jesus upon Himself. He said, "I am the resurrection, and the life: he that believeth in me, though he were dead, yet shall he live: and whosoever liveth and believeth in me shall never die." Again He said, "Because I live, ye shall live also." And again, "Ye believe in God, believe also in me." Our hope of immortality is based on Christ alone and not upon any desires, longings, arguments from analogy, or the instinct of immortality; and yet the hope of immortality which is revealed in Christ agrees with all those great desires and instincts.

There is, first of all, the idea of the instinct of immortality. The idea was there before Christ came. Paul did not say that Jesus discovered or invented the idea of immortality, but that He "brought life and immortality to light through the gospel." What before was in the shadow was now brought to light and shone forth in the clear light of the Christian revelation. The very idea of immortality is a mighty and unanswerable argument for the reality of it. Where could man, who is just a creature of the dust, get this sublime idea of immortal existence if there is no such existence? What put it into his mind? Man is the only creature who entombs his dead. Every grave, from the colossal pyramids which cast their shadow over the sands of Egypt to the flat stone in a quiet Presbyterian churchyard on the hills of western Pennsylvania, is an eloquent witness to the idea and instinct of everlasting life. No clever arguments can ever dismiss or invalidate this instinct. Through the ages man has clung to the idea of a future life. He lives in a vast cemetery, surrounded by dead races, dead empires, dead civilizations, and with death sweeping every generation of mankind over the falls of time into the abyss of eternity, and yet he has clung to the hope of immortal life. "The intuition of immortality is written in the heart of man by a Hand that writes no falsehoods."

Here sits he shaping wings to fly;
His heart forbodes a mystery;
He names the name Eternity.
                              —Tennyson, "Two Voices"

Again, the revelation of a future life by Jesus confirms man's belief in justice. "Shall not the Judge of all the earth do right?" And it has never seemed right to man that Elijah and Jezebel, Herod and John the Baptist, Paul and Nero, should in the end fare just the same, and that that common fate should be annihilation.

What Jesus taught confirms man's thought about the incompleteness of this life and the necessity of another life to give full expression and development to the talents and gifts that are in man. Bacon has an essay "Concerning Fame." It is only a fragment, and at the end of the essay we read in brackets, "The rest was not finished." That is a comment which, so far as this world is concerned, could well be written at the end of the chapter of every man's life, "The rest was not finished." In the cathedral at Toledo you can see paintings of the apostles by the great painter El Greco. Some of them are unfinished, and all that one sees is the barest outline—just a hand or a foot or a part of the head. That is all that man does in this life. He leaves just a sketch, an outline, of what might have been done, of what he planned to do. Man's intellectual and moral endowments are on a scale immeasurably larger than the needs of this present life. Only immortality and the greatness of immortality can ever satisfy the interminable longings of man's soul after nobler and higher things. How grandly Paul struck that note when he reminded the Romans that it was their high calling to "seek for glory and honor and immortality, eternal life."

But most of all, what Jesus revealed about the future life confirms and satisfies the affections of man's heart. "The heart," Pascal said, "has reasons that the mind knows nothing of." John tells us how, on the morning of the resurrection, Mary Magdalene "stood without at the sepulchre weeping." She was longing to see again the loved form of her Master. Only what Christ is and did and said can satisfy the loving, longing heart and wipe away all tears from the eyes of those who mourn. The recollection of departed friends is good, but the hope of meeting them again is better. The sunset glow is good, but better far the golden light of the radiant morning and the unclouded dawn. It is Christ, and Christ alone, who satisfies and confirms the deep instincts and desires and reasonings and affections of man's mind and heart.

THE NATURE OF THE LIFE TO COME

It is more the fact and the power and the glory of the life to come, than the nature of it, of which Christ and the Bible speak. At first that may strike you as strange. Why, you say, since it is so great and all-important a truth, are we not told more about the nature of that life? The fact is that we know as much now, revealed to us by Christ and the Scriptures, as it is possible for us to know in our present state. After Paul was caught up into paradise, speaking of that great experience, he said that he heard and saw things "which it is not lawful for a man to utter." That may well mean that the things he saw were so wonderful that he could not communicate them to others.

It is undoubtedly true also that more knowledge about the life to come would not give us greater comfort or greater warning than the knowledge which we now possess. When the rich man in hell desired of Abraham that he should send Lazarus to preach to his five godless brothers, Abraham said, "If they hear not Moses and the prophets, neither will they be persuaded, though one rose from the dead." In other words, a fuller knowledge of the life to come, both of heaven and of the place of the lost, would have no practical effect upon our life here.

Many of the descriptions of the heavenly life in the Bible are on the negative side. Rather than what is there, they tell us what is *not* there. But how great and comforting are those negatives, and what a world that will be of which you can say what the Bible says of it, that there shall be no more curse, that is, no more sin, and no more death, which is the wages of sin, for sin and death always ride together in this world; and no more sea, the symbol of the unrest of life; and no more pain; no groan of misery shall be heard by day and no cry of agony shall break the silence of the night; and no more sorrow or crying. How great is the capacity of the human heart for sorrow! Even Jesus, who took our nature upon Him, was "a man of sorrows, and acquainted with grief." But there God shall wipe away all tears from their eyes. And now comes the sublime climax to all those negative descriptions of heaven, "The gates of it shall not be shut at all by day: *for there shall be no night there.*" Which means there shall be no more night of sin, no more night of pain, no more night of sorrow, and no more night of death.

On the positive side we are not left without great assurance. One of the most helpful things said on the positive side about the nature of the heavenly life is what the apostle Paul said in his great chapter on the resurrection of the body and the immortality of the soul, "As we have borne the image of the earthy, we shall also bear the image of the heavenly." Here we have had an image of the earthy, perfectly adapted to the needs of this life. There we shall bear the image of the heavenly, perfectly and beautifully adapted to the needs of that life. Paul further explains what he means by "the image of the heavenly" by telling us that Christ was "the firstfruits of them that slept." Just as the first sheaf of wheat or the first leaf on the tree or the first fruits of the vine are like every other sheaf and leaf and fruit which are to follow, so Christ in His resurrection was the first fruits, the pattern, the sample, the model of the believer's resurreciton life and body.

This lets us know that the image of the heavenly will be the image of a redeemed and glorified body. To make the Christian hope of immortality mean just the survival of the spirit is to evacuate the force of the New Testament's reiterated teaching as to the ideal sanctity of the body. What we believe in is what we say in the Apostle's Creed, "the resurrection of the body *and* the life everlasting." Let no one discount or look with disdain upon his body, for the body is "fearfully and wonderfully made," made in the image of God. What a faithful and obedient servant the body is, even here in this state of limitation and under the shadow and bondage of sin! How perfectly and immediately it gives expression to every emotion of the heart of man—shame, joy, pain, fear, sorrow, love, hope! If the body can do that, even here in this present state, then what will it be like when the body has been redeemed and united to a redeemed soul! That is what the apostle meant when he said, "It is sown a natural body; it is raised a spiritual body." And again, "It is sown in corruption; it is raised in incorruption. It is sown in dishonor; it is raised in glory."

The image of the heavenly will be the image of righteousness and holiness. Here the whole creation is under the shadow of sin, hence the civil war and discord within our breast, and the passions which lodge in our hearts like evil beasts in a den. But when all this is no more, when our souls no longer cleave to the dust, when men naturally love what God loves, when the whole legion of evil spirits has been cast out of man and he sits clothed and in his right mind at the foot of the Creator— all that God had in mind when He said, "Let us make man in our image"—then what will it be like! If, as Jesus said, the holy angels rejoice and sing over one sinner that repenteth, what they are rejoicing and singing over is not merely what man has been delivered *from*, but what he has been restored *to*—the glorious image of God.

Once more, the image of the heavenly will be the image of high achievement and great enterprise. The one particular clue which Jesus gave us as to the nature of the heavenly life was what He told the Sadducees who asked Him that foolish question about a woman who had survived seven husbands. Jesus said that in the resurrection they are "as the angels of God in heaven." We do not know a great deal about the angels; but we know this, that they are mighty in intelligence, sinless in their character, armed with great powers, and that they go forth to minister on behalf of God unto them who shall be the heirs of salvation. This lets us know that if we are to be like the angels, we shall have great work to do in heaven and great joy in the doing of it. What have Elijah and Isaiah been doing since they ended their great ministry on earth? What has David been doing since he hung up his harp for the last time on earth? What has John been doing since he painted his last picture of the heavenly life and the New Jerusalem and the sea of glass mingled with fire? What has Paul been doing since, there by the pyramid of Caestius, the headsman's axe flashed in the sun and he put on immortality? The only answer that we can give is that great answer of the New Testament, "His servants shall serve him: and they shall see his face; and his name shall be in their foreheads."

Finally, the image of the heavenly will be the image of great joy. There was joy in heaven and on earth when man was created, for all the morning stars sang together and the sons of God shouted for joy. Christ came to restore to man his lost joy. In the heavenly life we shall taste again the true joy which belongs to the sons of God. In the words of the great psalm, "Thou wilt show me the path of life: in thy presence is fulness of joy; at thy right hand there are pleasures for evermore."

A precious cup of that joy will be the joy of reunion with our friends. Thomas Carlyle, in the beautiful essay written after the death of his father, expressed for us all that desire and hope and joy of reunion in another world, "And now, beloved father, farewell for the last time in this world of shadows! In the world of reality may the Great Father again bring us together in perfect holiness and perfect love. Amen."

Paul told the Thessalonians that they were not to mourn as those who had no hope, and he comforted their hearts with the hope of meeting again their friends who had passed into the shadow and silence of death. Moses and Elijah, one dead for fourteen hundred years and the other translated for nine hundred years, appeared in glory, in the full power of their personality, on the Mount of Transfiguration. Jesus comforted His disciples when He was about to be taken from them by telling them that He was going to prepare a place for them, that where He was there they might be also. Without recognition and reunion there would have been no comfort in that assurance. And last of all, and most beautiful of all, is what Jesus said to that poor thief and robber on the cross who asked Him to remember him when He came into His Kingdom, "Today shalt thou be *with me* in paradise." This leaves us in no doubt as to the reunion with our friends in the kingdom of the blessed.

When the New Testament comes to speak of this great

change from death to life and life to death, it employs a number of beautiful metaphors and figures of speech. One is that of sleep. Jesus said of the daughter of Jairus and of Lazarus—loved Lazarus—that they were not dead but sleeping. He did not mean that they had not actually died, but that He was going to awaken them out of the sleep of death, for He said of Lazarus, "I go, that I may awake him out of sleep." So Christ by the power of His resurrection awakens His beloved out of the sleep of death.

Another metaphor is that of the Exodus, the going out. Moses and Elijah on the Mount spake with Jesus of His exodus, His death, which He should accomplish at Jerusalem. Just as the children of Israel made their exodus out of the land of Egypt and out of the house of bondage into the land of Canaan, so out of the bondage and limitations of this life by the gateway of death we make our exodus into the heavenly kingdom.

Another figure is that of the tent and the house. Paul said, "If our earthly house of this tabernacle"—literally "this tent"—"were dissolved, we have a building of God, an house not make with hands, eternal in the heavens." Our life here in the body is like living in a tent. The tent is frail; the adverse winds of life can blow it over. But at death we exchange the fragile tent for the house which is permanent, a building from God, a house not made with hands, eternal in the heavens.

Still another metaphor was that employed by Paul when he himself was about to pass through this great change from life to death. Writing his last message from the prison at Rome, he said, "I am now ready to be offered, and the time of my departure is at hand"—literally "the time for the sailing of the ship." Just as the ship weighs anchor and hoists its sails and sets out across the sea for the unseen haven beyond the horizon, so at death the believer sets sail for the heavenly shore.

But most familiar, I suppose, and most precious to us all is that figure of speech employed by our Savior when He likened this change to that of going home. "In my Father's house are many mansions. . . . I go to prepare a place for you." If you were brought up in a good Christian home, you can remember how it was that you thought to yourself that home must be heaven. But as the years go by and the earthly home is broken up and the members of the family move on into the next world, we begin to realize that heaven is home. That is the home which God has prepared for you. That is the home which is suited for your immortal soul, made in the image of God. That you might have a right and a title to that home, Christ died for you on the cross. Do not forget that home! Do not miss that home! May we all at length get home!

OTHER BOOKS BY CLARENCE E. MACARTNEY

Chariots of Fire

Drawing upon colorful yet lesser-known characters of the Old and New Testaments, Dr. Clarence Macartney presents eighteen powerful and timeless sermons. One of America's greatest biographical preachers, Macartney's sermons aim for the common heart of human experience. Each sermon contains a wealth of illustrations and quotations that add depth and insight to the exposition. *Chariots of Fire* is eye-opening, biblical exposition from one of America's premier preachers and makes an inspiring devotional or study resource.

ISBN 0-8254-3274-x   **192 pp.**   **paperback**

Great Women of the Bible

A collection of sermons from a master pulpiteer of yesterday. Macartney's unique descriptive style brings these women of the Bible to life and provides inspirational reading for all Christians.

ISBN 0-8254-3268-5   **208 pp.**   **paperback**

Greatest Texts of the Bible

This collection of sermons represents some of the author's strongest and most impassioned preaching. Except for slight modifications and updating, and the insertion of Scripture references where needed, these sermons are reissued in their original form.

ISBN 0-8254-3266-9   **208 pp.**   **paperback**

He Chose Twelve

This careful study of the New Testament illuminates the personality and individuality of each of the Twelve Disciples. A carefully crafted series of Bible character sketches including chapters on all the apostles as well as Paul and John the Baptist.

ISBN 0-8254-3270-7   **176 pp.**   **paperback**

Paul the Man

Macartney delves deeply into Paul's background and heritage, helping twentieth-century Christians understand what made him the pivotal figure of New Testament history. Paul, the missionary and theologian, is carefully traced in this insightful work.

ISBN 0-8254-3269-3   **208 pp.**   **paperback**

Strange Texts but Grand Truths

Drawing upon seventeen striking and unusual texts of Scripture, Dr. Clarence Macartney utilizes the natural curiosity aroused by the unfamiliar to expound the important and practical truths of God's Word. Macartney brings to life overlooked lessons from biblical passages. Each sermon contains a wealth of illustrations and quotations that add depth and insight to the exposition of one of America's premier preachers, making this volume an inspiring devotional or study resource.

ISBN 0-8254-3272-3   **192 pp.**   **paperback**

Twelve Great Questions About Christ
Macartney addresses commonly asked questions about the life and person of Jesus Christ. The integrity of the Scriptures underlies the provocative answers that Dr. Macartney provides in this thoughtful book. The broad range of subject matter will inform and inspire laymen and clergy alike.

ISBN 0-8254-3267-7   **160 pp.**   **paperback**

Available from Christian Bookstores, or

kregel
PUBLICATIONS

P. O. Box 2607 • Grand Rapids, MI 49501